The SERENDIPITY COOKBOOK

The SERENDIPITY COOKBOOK

by PAT MILLER

with CALVIN HOLT and STEPHEN BRUCE

illustrated by PAT MILLER

A CITADEL PRESS BOOK

Published by Carol Publishing Group

A Citadel Press Book
Published by Carol Publishing Group
Citadel Press is a registered trademark of Carol Communications, Inc.
Editorial Offices: 600 Madison Avenue, New York, N.Y. 10022
Sales and Distribution Offices: 120 Enterprise Avenue, Secaucus, N.J.
 07094
In Canada: Canadian Manda Group, P.O. Box 920, Station U, Toronto,
 Ontario M8Z 5P9
Queries regarding rights and permissions should be addressed to Carol
 Publishing Group, 600 Madison Avenue, New York, N.Y. 10022

Carol Publishing Group books are available at special discounts for
bulk purchases, for sales promotions, fund-raising, or educational
purposes. Special editions can be created to specifications. For details,
contact Special Sales Department, Carol Publishing Group, 120
Enterprise Avenue, Secaucus, N.J. 07094

Manufactured in the United States of America
10 9 8 7 6 5 4 3 2 1

Library of Congress Cataloging-in-Publication Data

Miller, Pat.
    The Serendipty cookbook : the best from New York's incredible
dessert emporium / by Pat Miller with Stephen Bruce and Calvin Holt.
    p. cm.
First published in New York by Wynwood Press in 1990—Pub. Info.
    ISBN 0-8065-1541-4 : $14.95
    1. Cookery.   2. Menus.   3. Serendipity (Restaurant) I. Bruce,
Stephen.   II. Holt, Calvin.   III. Serendipity (Restaurant)
IV. Title.
TX714.M554   1994
641.5—dc20
                                                          94-20351
                                                             CIP

To Sir Horace Walpole,
who invented serendipity;
to Calvin, Stephen, and Patch,
who reinvented it

A Serendipity cookbook? Wow!
—Andy Warhol

Table of Contents

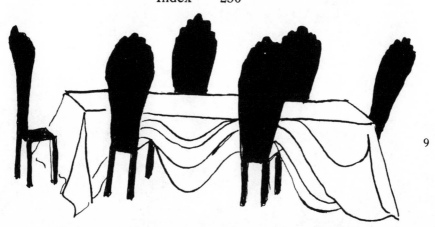

9

Acknowledgments

I want to thank all the ghosts of Serendipity past, without whose inspiration there could be no *Serendipity Cookbook*. That includes James Beard, Anita Loos, Miss Milton, Miss Julia, and Mrs. Kalibash, wherever you are.

I'm indebted to Bill Thompson, our publisher, and Jerry Perles, our agent. Without them, the Serendipity saga might never have seen the light of day.

Special thanks to all those friends of Serendipity who believed in this project, and gave it their moral support through its darkest hours.

Federico Suro, Martin Beck, Chris Lione, Bobby Short, Carol Baker, Leo Lerman, and Lynn Dubal for dishy quotes and anecdotes; Rhoda Schlamm, who taught me how to propose to a publisher so he wouldn't say no; Tom O'Donnell for brightening the embryonic phase of this enterprise; Mario Cardillo for constructive criticism and family recipes; John Walsh of Nesle's for the maharajah's chandelier; George and Paul Gorra of Agora for vintage saloon doors; Paul Davis of Dept. 56 for the best Aunt Jemima cookie jar in town; Daisy and Milt, and Peggy and Steve; the libraries of the Metropolitan Museum, Cooper-Hewitt, Condé Nast, and the New York Public Library for rare glimpses under Tiffany lamps, beneath the Third Avenue El, and into Kennedy's Camelot and Reich's Orgone Box.

Most of all, I'm grateful to Stephen Bruce and Calvin Holt for keeping the pleasantly unexpected frozen hot, even on Sunday.

PM

11

The Saga Continues

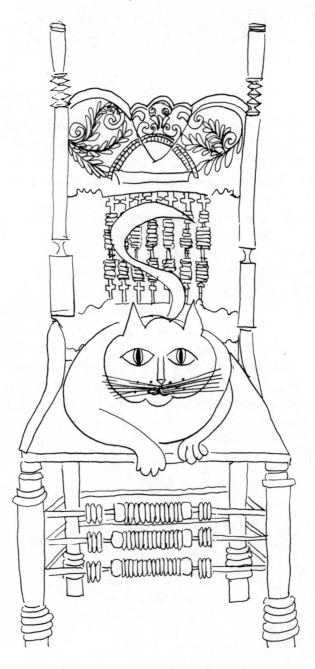

Serendipity! The art of finding the pleasantly unexpected by chance or by sagacity. Invented by eighteenth-century wordsmith Sir Horace Walpole.

"Hey," said the boys, "that's a good name for a place of our own." The rest reads like *A Thousand and One Nights*. They pooled their entire fortune of three hundred dollars and staked a claim to a tiny principality in the basement of a tenement on East 58th Street.

It was New York's first coffeehouse boutique. The first Tiffany lamp-shaded meeting place since the days of Diamond Jim Brady. Serendipity had come into the world four tables, sixteen chairs, and a towering espresso machine strong. In no time, patrons outnumbered the facilities. Nightly the line formed, stretching around the block and under the old Third Avenue El.

Before he was anyone, Andy Warhol declared it his favorite sweetshop, and paid his chits in drawings. Photographers discovered the charms of Tiffany glass set against whitewashed walls. New York's avant-garde caught on that nineteenth-century junk was suddenly twentieth-century chic.

The princes lost no time learning how to cook, design, whip, and turn on the frozen hots. They rolled in the loot and rolled around the corner to the cozy brownstone on Serendipity Street. The entire Silk Stocking community squeezed into designer jeans and queued up.

The kitchen buzzed to all hours producing never-before extravaganzas. The general store and boutique grew trendier with every passing Hebrew Eyechart dishtowel and Little Red Riding Hood's jigsaw puzzle (365 pieces, all of them red). Swivel-hipped waiters balanced trays overflowing with calories. Everything was for sale. Frozen Hot Chocoholics were nurtured and Apricot Smushniks were sated. Palates pampered with caviar developed a lust for Hard Times fare like Lemon Ice Box Pie and Texas Chili.

James Beard tasted and tested in the Serendipity kitchen. *Vogue* editors planned their issues at old-fashioned kitchen tables, deciding tomorrow's in and outs. Hundred-dollar-an-hour models nibbled on watercress while movie stars left forkprints in whipped cream mountains. Before she was First Lady, Jackie O. discovered she was pregnant. Between sips of cappuccino, she spotted an appealing gingham Baby Doll "mumu" at a modest fifteen dollars. "I'll take it," enthused Jackie, "in every color."

Vogue gave Stephen a full page on his mumu, calling it "the perfect dress when you're *en famille*." Sarahdipity, the cat-in-residence, thought so, too. She snatched a mumu off its hanger and made a bed of it in a semiprivate nook somewhere near the cash register. There, on the busiest Saturday night in kingdom come, she gave birth to five of the most adoptable kittens in town.

"Fun is hard work," pouted Brigitte Bardot in Roger Vadim's film *And God Created Woman*. The Serendipity 3 agreed as they toiled to keep their perpetual house party going full tilt, full-time, seven days a week. Patch played "The Man with a Pan," as he wielded omelettes from a special bar in the rear of the dining room. Often, he got egg on his face and on his best black suit as well. Calvin, in his Teddy Roosevelt pince-nez, lampooned Patch's Ashley Wilkes performance as he dished out more ham than omelettes, alongside him. Back in the kitchen, he skinned himself alive "mushing" peaches for a confection called Peach Mush, while loudly complaining that he was the galley slave while his partners took their ease on center stage like a pair of prima donnas.

It wasn't so. The Man with a Pan led a double life. By night he slaved as a songwriter and lyricist. Stephen Bruce stepped out of his couturier role and onto a blistering tar roof to tie-dye, sun-bleach, splatter-paint, sweat, and toil in putting together his newest fashion show.

In this tableau, everyone played a part. Inconsequential busboys looked like cherubic bambinos who stepped out of a Caravaggio canvas just to charm the ladies who lunch. Hosts who did the greeting and seating were cast with care. To be led to a table by a dead ringer for Brideshead's Lord Flyte was an exhilarating experience. Being swept to a seat by the embodiment of southern gallantry seemed a waltz away from a St. Cecilia Ball in Charleston.

Waiters were encouraged to cultivate "controlled eccentricity," to be attentive, courteous to a fault, but as outrageous as the law would allow. They regularly splashed their three-piece Sunday suits, the required dress code, as they hand-whipped cream and custom-decorated desserts as whim dictated. They went to extreme lengths. One day, three French women came in with hair dyed chartreuse, orange, and fuchsia, respectively. The waiter, Chris Lioni, now head art director of *Arts & Antiques* magazine, dipped into Easter egg dyes, coordinating the whipped cream on their sundaes to match their hair.

The house rule firmly stated that waiters had to be chorus-boy slim. Whipped cream and hot fudge must never cross their hips. Chris became a calorie junkie and was warned to lose ten pounds, or else. Desperate, he squeezed into a tight girdle and said no to cakes, pies, and chocolate rather than say good-bye to Serendipity.

Peter Geraldo, a waiter who doubled as a fashion artist and amateur impersonator, would wait until after the lunch rush was over to entertain the staff with the songs of Marlene Dietrich. His signature piece was "In the Ruins of Berlin." One afternoon, he was called upon to entertain none other than the boss, Calvin. Peter obliged with Gloria Swanson's mad scene from *Sunset Boulevard*. As he descended the spiral stairway, expostulating in millifluent tones, "I'm ready, Mr. de Mille," who should be standing at the foot of the stairs but La Swanson, in the flesh. The Hollywood legend laughingly cheered him on, but didn't offer to get him a screen test.

Penny Green was one of Peter's chosen customers. At least three times a week, she and her three Shih Tzus arrived for lunch. The ritual never varied. Each dog would be served a bowl of water with a maraschino cherry floating in it.

Not to be outdone, Patch brought his favorite Conover model, Carol Taylor, an antique coal scuttle to place her newborn daughter in. It was those personal, original touches that made people and pets feel so pampered, so much at home.

Not all the staff were on payroll. For the love of Serendipity, Lynn Dubal, a striking teenager long of leg and false eyelashes, slipped into one of Stephen Bruce's creations and showed it to great advantage as she strolled amongst the tables during lunchtime. She sold the dress off her back and repeated the performance as a steady solo fashion show, modeling dresses with names like Olive Oyl and Tondalayo. This led to real fashion shows staged by Lynn's mother, Edith Berke, a professional fashion coordinator. Edith collaborated with Patch in writing the commentary. Calvin, the official commentator, kept audience hilarity in high gear.

Act Two of the daily floor show was supplied by another volunteer, "Rollerena," the whirling dervish on roller skates. A gifted street showman who made guest appearances on TV, he would skate into Serendipity at lunchtime, vanish into the gents' room to change into a wedding gown, then skate out to execute daredevil spins in between waiters balancing overflowing trays of food. The entire audience held its collective breath until he would disappear into thin air as mysteriously as he had arrived.

Celebrity-watching was a sport in itself. Habitués had their favorite tables.

Cove Two was reserved for its regular occupant, Marilyn Monroe. She would arrive of an afternoon while her chauffeur waited at the curb. Though a universally recognized sex goddess, she was at heart timid, and rather virginal. She hid behind dark glasses and a raincoat as she indulged in her favorite pastime, Miss Milton's Lovely Fudge Pie. A *Vogue* editor wondered what Monroe wore under her coat, and one day, she asked her. "Chanel Number Five," came the whispered reply.

Andy Warhol held court at the Rose Table, so named for its rose-embossed Tiffany shade. Though he is now considered almost the only artist to have achieved stardom of such magnitude in his lifetime, Andy's first "gallery" was Serendipity. He remained faithful to its hot fudge sundaes to the end. In the beginning, his drawings covered every square inch of wall space in the tiny 58th Street cafe, and even hung on the ceiling. Suzie Frankfort, an early collector, bought his butterflies and flowers for twenty-five dollars each, and asked for an introduction. When they met, it was love at first sight. Soon they became collaborators on the cookbook *Wild Raspberries,* an esoteric undertaking for those who prefer to cook with their eyes.

Andy came each night with an entourage of dévotees. As he drew the feet of the rich and famous, his followers hand-colored them. They did the same with the illustrations for his hand-bound books, *Fairies at the Bottom of My Garden* and *Twenty-Five Cats Named Sam and One Blue Pussy.* Both books made the best-seller list at Serendipity book-signing parties that followed, with his mother, Julia, on hand to supply his unique signature.

Sundaes and celebrities weren't the only things that drew Andy to Serendipity night after night. He was hopelessly smitten with Stephen, a charismatic young man whose Sheik-of-Araby looks held a faint trace of country boy innocence. On Valentine's Day, Andy made drawings of his obsession from every angle, hearts darting from eyes, ears, and mouth. He gave them to Stephen as a gift that will one day outshine Tiffany in value.

Andy wanted to be the first to have the "Serendipity look," the white walls, nineteenth-century oak furniture and Tiffany lamps. He commissioned the boys to decorate his apartment. Calvin had just installed a Tiffany lamp in Andy's house on a "tryout" basis. Suddenly, word came through the decorators' grapevine that the distinguished antique dealer Lillian Nassau was beginning to see Tiffany in a new light since the Serendipity revival. That meant prices were about to go through the ceiling.

Calvin's amusing twenty-five-dollar revival would soon be worth far more than the modest price he'd quoted Andy, already an avid collector. He rushed to Andy's house to retrieve his shade and return it to Serendipity, where it hangs to this day. Out of pique, Andy gave up sundaes for a week or two, but his sweet tooth got the best of him. Years later, when the Italian film producer Lina Wertmuller bought up half the "Tiffany" in Serendipity, she tried to buy "Andy's shade," too, but was turned down.

Andy had plenty of subjects for his "Celebrity Feet" drawings in this wall-to-wall Grauman's Theater* of famous feet. The well-shod inseparables, Helen Hayes, Anita Loos, and Lillian Gish were always present, as were Leonard Bernstein, Jerome Robbins, Paulette Goddard, Gloria Swanson, and Gloria Vanderbilt in a pink Mainbocher and clouds of Fracas perfume. She ordered twenty Mainbocher pink topiaries from Stephen to send to her dearest friends at Christmas. Gloria, the toast of fashion, was honored with the creation of Pink Ice, an item that is still a feature on the menu. Thus she was, to Serendipity, what Nellie Melba was to Escoffier when he created Melba Toast and Pêche Melba.

The score from *My Fair Lady* played on the new LPs while the designer of its sets and costumes, Cecil Beaton, celebrated at Serendipity with Tennessee Williams and Truman Capote. Perhaps he was waiting for his elusive muse, Greta Garbo, who sometimes came in in her slouch-brimmed hat. The glitterati were well represented, and for contrast, you could always find a sprinkling of little old lavender-haired ladies from Queens and Long Island.

One of Serendipity's charms was its democratic attitude. The nobodies were given the same treatment as the somebodies. They, too, had to wait their turn in line. The most memorable of the little old somebodies was Marianne Moore, Brooklyn's poet laureate in her Revolutionary War general's cocked hat. She was seen often, except during baseball season. Miss Moore, an avid Yankees fan, wouldn't miss her team's games for anything, not even a cup of piping hot Serendip.

Vogue's Leo Lerman remembers being one of the first to beat the drums for Serendipity. "Going down those rickety stairs," he recalls, "was like descending into some extraordinary cave of wonders." He says, "They were true pioneers. They had the most marvelous things to buy. Junk, but very good junk." He credits them with inventing a form of shop which has influenced merchandising all over the world. The very first week after its opening,

* Now Mann's Chinese Theater

Lerman, then feature editor of *Mademoiselle*, had spread the news to the entire staff. Editors came trooping in, and with them, photographers. "The first thing I bought in Serendipity was a watch fob," says Lerman. "It was very expensive. It cost five dollars."

Spoiled New Yorkers were mesmerized. Serendipity was the first to combine food and objects. The menu was always a little boy's dream. Lerman proudly escorted his personal luminary, Marlene Dietrich, a big boy's dream in black leather. "It got to be a place where you saw everybody who, at that moment, was somebody, everybody who thought he was going to be somebody, and eventually people who came to watch these people." Lerman continued, "Their wonderful flair, the extraordinary imagination and strong, extroverted personalities of these three young men were a magnet."

To be fair, Serendipity was born not in 1954, but in any year you care to guess, when its three founders drew their first breaths.

Calvin Holt danced out of the birth canal singing the overture from *To Catch a Star*, and landed in an Arkansas cotton patch. He was all mischief and electric blue eyes. At the sight of him, grown men and women behaved like mushballs. A strong-willed Taurus, this indulged princeling was anointed king and supreme ruler, even as he lay in the cradle. As a tender tot, he ran the only cotton gin within 100 miles and was unanimously elected mayor of Hazen, Arkansas, population 500, where he presided with a little help from his grandpa.

Preston Caradine issued forth in a grand old four-poster in the middle of a fudge pie plantation. A little wordsmith from Little Rock, they say he came into the world spouting Noel Coward song lyrics. The doting Caradines, given to noms de plume, called him "Patch" after the brightest square on the family quilt. While other toddlers were playing patty cakes, this prodigy was teaching his Aunt Buba and his sister, Miss Milton, how to bake the real thing. Under his tutelage, the summerhouse cake rose higher, the sand tarts were richer, and the fudge pie was beyond compare.

Stephen Bruce's arrival was perhaps the greatest enigma of all. His eyes with their mysterious Slavic tilt, the dimple in his chin, and his dark, silky hair bore little resemblance to Mummy and Daddy Bruce. Evasively, the senior Bruces insisted that the stork brought him. But rumor has it his natural parents were Pola Negri and Rudolph Valentino. Whatever his eugenics, this infant phenomenon said to his stunned mother, "Hand me those pins, Mums," and proceeded to design his own christening hat.

These three kids from out of nowhere crossed paths over an ice-cream soda on Broadway, or was it at a ballet barre in Carnegie Hall? Before you could say Serendipity 3, they found themselves in the nether regions of 234 East 58th Street painting dank basement walls Lady Mendl white, hanging up junk they found in garbage heaps: bright-hued glass lampshades, old, broken-down kitchen chairs of pre-Depression vintage which they mended and painted. Up went an ancient espresso machine with a bronze eagle on its top. As they slaved happily away, philistines shook their heads. "It won't work," they said. "It's hard enough to run one business. You've got two, a boutique and a coffeehouse. It's never been done. No capital. No business experience. No liquor license. Forget it. New York eats kids like you for breakfast. Save yourself a lot of grief and go back home where you belong."

"What makes it even harder is your crazy name," sneered a troublemaker. "Who can pronounce it? Who can spell it? What the devil does it mean?"

"That's for us to know and you to find out," was their defiant retort, and they gaily went about hanging up their shingle with its crazily beguiling name.

The year 1954 was a terrific time to start the impossible. Phone calls were a nickel. Postage stamps were three cents. A taxi ride anywhere in town was a dollar, including the tip. And a five-cent ride on the Third Avenue "El" could take them down to the Bowery, a treasure trove of cheap chic, where finds like white ironstone restaurant china could be picked up for a pittance and sold at a profit.

Café society frolicked in a few bright pools, El Morocco, the Blue Angel, the Colony, "21", the Stork Club. They laughed with Mike Nichols and Elaine May, Mort Sahl, and Woody Allen. They cried with Edith Piaf and Billie Holiday. In Lou Walters' Latin Quarter, they watched Calvin dance the fandango while girls ran around in G-strings with bananas on their heads. One night, Calvin took a snooze under a table and Walters fired him. Did he care? Not a bit. He gave himself a rousing bon voyage party and invited all the "gypsy" dancers. Then he and his friends set about planning their venture.

This is how things were in the world they would soon plunge into. The ladies who shopped the Fifth Avenue stores worked up a real appetite for lunch. They nourished themselves at Schrafft's, the Colony, Hamburg Heaven, or Kirby Allen, a little Madison Avenue restaurant owned by two maiden ladies where the menu offered cottage pudding and "Lasagne, A Very Interesting Italian Dish." The time had come for omelettes and casseroles and crepes.

At the fabled gastronomy palace, The Chambord, dinner for two with Dom

Perignon came to $100. This luxury coexisted in the shadow of the El with P. J. Clarke's, the dying turn-of-the-century Irish saloon resuscitated by Ray Milland's movie *The Lost Weekend*, which was now packing them in for beer and burgers. Other popular Third Avenue hangouts were The Original Joe's and Bickford's, where New York went slumming. Here, a dollar bought a whole dinner. Soon that same dollar would take you away from the liver-and-onions or a couple of beers to the other side of the looking glass.

If Calvin had any qualms about the wisdom of their new plan, he could confer with his own personal swami, the Orgone Box, which he kept in the run-down loft he shared with dancer Merce Cunningham, an out-of-tune piano, and two talented graduates of Cooper Union, Milton Glaser and Seymour Chwast. Wilhelm Reich's contemplation box was supposed to cure sexual inhibitions and evoke orgasm by releasing orgone energy.* For the repressed, who sat in it naked and concentrated, it offered hope. For Calvin, it was the height of chic.

Chwast, a baby of eighteen, was tongue-tied before man-of-the-world Calvin and his mysterious box. One day, the box began to emit smoke. Chwast flew into the street below in panic. Soon, the whole loft was enveloped in flames. Calvin, fortunately, was perched on a ladder at East 58th Street, out of harm's way and brushing fresh white oil paint over grime-covered walls.

That same morning, September 14, Stephen Bruce's mother woke up in Constableville, New York, shrieking, "I had a dream. My boy will become a prince." The family doctor gave her a sedative and advised a psychiatrist. That night, a telegram arrived, delivered by Western Union, telling her about the opening of Serendipity 3, kingdom of the three princes of Serendip. Mrs. Bruce thereafter was looked upon as something of a clairvoyant and was frequently consulted by the doctor, the psychiatrist, and the town mayor.

Serendipity held its housewarming for twenty friends on Sunday, September 15. The still-wet white oil paint covered everything, including the overhead boiler pipe that heated the basement. As the first guests arrived, steam came gushing up through the paint and they were greeted with the smell of a swamp in a heat wave. The pristine white paint turned a bilious yellow.

* In 1954 (not a terrific year for Wilhelm Reich), the U.S. government prohibited the sale of his boxes. In 1956, Reich was convicted of violating the injunctions and sentenced to a prison term in Lewisburg, where he died in 1957.

The princes turned red. But they needn't have concerned themselves. As they say in show business, the audience loves a fluff.

Soon everyone was killing to get in, past the garbage cans. Café society thought it amusing to stand in line, waiting for the six café tables to be free. Stars of Hollywood and Broadway, socialites, cover girls, celebrity authors, artists, playwrights, designers, producers, decorators and ingenues thought it great fun to stand in line in the kitchen waiting an eternity for the WC with its old-fashioned pull-chain. How chic, how original to sign autographs for the cook and kitchen help while waiting. Everything was a delight: the giant chemist's beaker on a pedestal, filled with Alka Seltzer for hangovers; the wooden hat tree abloom with 1920s cloches; the whipped cream–peaked espressos and cappuccinos served with such style, form and dash by what to all appearances were Victorian gentlemen out of the nineteenth century.

The wrecker's ball hit the old El in 1955. By May 12, it went the way of many of New York's brownstone row houses and Sanford White palaces. The canyon of Third Avenue, always shrouded in darkness, revealed a wealth of antique shops, old Irish taverns and cold water flats that rented for thirty-five and forty dollars a month. When this poor man's heaven came to light, its days were numbered. To Serendipity, it represented a junk mine that they could transmute by alchemy into pure gold.

Post–World War II fashions pinioned women into Merry Widow bras and girdles. Men were buttoned into three-piece Brooks Brothers suits and uniform white Oxford shirts. Conformity was in. Even the colors you wore were decreed as if by a holy commandment. Harmonious colors were "good taste." Clashing colors were "bad taste." Such rigidity hadn't been seen since the Dark Ages.

Gays played it straight at the job. After five, they headed for the Oak Bar at the Plaza, where Fifth Avenue "ribbon clerks" and the more effete midtown office workers could pick up new friends from an endless ocean of likely candidates in Oxford gray Brooks Brothers uniforms. In time, it became all too painfully apparent to the hotel and its stuffier guests that the venerable Oak Room had become a "den of fairies," as one dowager put it. A pink "dismissal" slip was issued to each gay patron with his bill. It said, "We are no longer interested in your patronage."

They retreated further into the closet. Purges by the House on Un-American Activities had driven other freewheeling, free-spirited creative types, notably writers and artists, into exile too. What was needed was a place where they could all loosen their restraints, where imagination ruled the roost. That place was Serendipity.

One East Side advertising executive, R.S., found freedom from restraint by leaving his conventional Brooks Brothers' powder blue boxer shorts home when he went out at night club-hopping. One evening there was an armed robbery at La Rue, one of his favorite watering holes. The men were forced to drop their trousers at gunpoint. He had (*continued on page 42*)

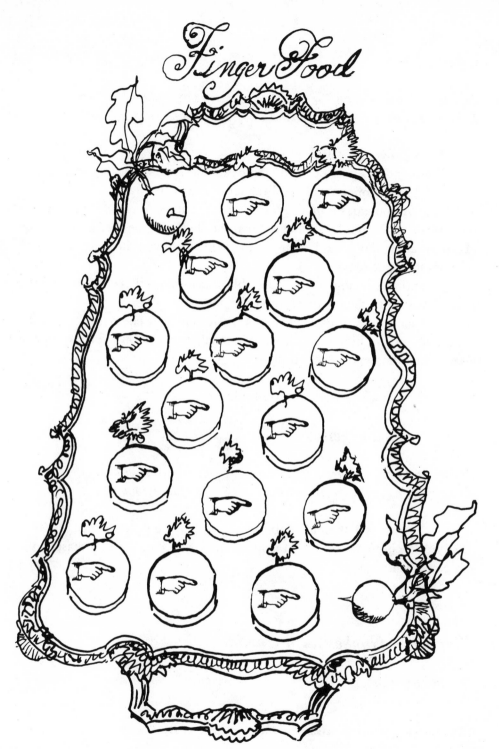

Spudnikettes

24 bite-sized new potatoes　　　　*1 cup shredded cheddar cheese*
Enough vegetable oil to cover potatoes　　*½ pound bacon, fried and crumbled*

1. Preheat oven to 350 degrees.
2. Wash and dry potatoes and arrange in one layer on baking sheets.
3. Bake for 30 minutes or until tender.
4. Remove potatoes from oven and cut into halves. Scoop out pulp with a melon-ball cutter, but be sure not to tear the shells. There should be only an eighth of an inch of pulp left inside the skin. Reserve pulp for another use (like mashed potatoes).
5. Heat the vegetable oil in a deep, black cast-iron skillet and deep-fry the potato skins until they are well browned and crisp.
6. Fill the inside of each potato skin with cheddar cheese and melt the cheese under the broiler. Sprinkle crumbled, fried bacon over the melted cheese and arrange on a round platter.

Serves 12 as an accompaniment to drinks.

Cleopatra's Bargettes

24 bite-sized new potatoes　　　　*1 cup dairy sour cream*
Enough vegetable oil to cover potatoes　　*8 ounces black caviar*

1. Follow steps 1 through 5 above to deep-fry the potato skins.
2. Fill each potato skin with a spoonful of sour cream and a teaspoon or more of caviar.

Serves 12.

Blue Corn Nachos with Cheddar

36 blue corn chips*　　　　*½ pound cheddar cheese, grated*

* Blue Heaven Corn Chips are available at Grace's Marketplace, 1237 Third Avenue, New York, NY.

1. Place corn chips on a cookie sheet and place a teaspoonful of grated cheddar on each.

2. Toast them under a broiler until the cheese melts. Serve them piping hot.

Serves 12 guests 3 each, but that is never enough.

Blue Corn Nachos with Goat Cheese

*36 blue corn chips**   *½ pound goat cheese*

1. Place corn chips on a cookie sheet and place a dab of goat cheese on each chip.

2. Toast them under a broiler until the cheese melts. Serve piping hot.

Serves 3 each to 12 guests, but they always ask for more.

Chicken Nachos

3 tablespoons butter
1 cup mushrooms, sliced
4 pounds of skinless, boneless chicken
   meat; dark and light; pre-cooked
   and cut into bite-sized pieces
¾ cup black olives, sliced

½ cup Italian parsley, chopped fine
1 cup Italian tomato paste
1½ cups salsa (recipe follows)
½ teaspoon cumin, or to taste
½ teaspoon salt, or to taste

1. In the skillet of a chafing dish, melt the butter and sauté the mushrooms lightly.

2. Add the chicken, olives, and parsley and mix well.

3. Add the tomato paste, salsa, cumin, and salt and mix thoroughly. Keep warm and serve over blue corn chips.*

Makes 36 nachos.

* Blue Heaven Corn Chips are available at Grace's Marketplace, 1237 Third Avenue, New York, NY.

Salsa

1 #2 can whole tomatoes
½ Spanish or Videlia onion, chopped
    fine
1 large, firm tomato, chopped fine

1 large, firm green pepper, chopped
    fine
½ cup jalapeño peppers, chopped fine
1 teaspoon salt, or to taste

1. Drain the canned tomatoes; reserve the juice. Chop the tomatoes fine and return to the juice.
2. Add the chopped onion, tomato, pepper, and jalapeñoes to the juice.
3. Add salt to taste, mix thoroughly. Use for Chicken Nachos (above), or serve, separately, with blue corn chips.

Makes 1½ cups.

Hot Crab, Artichoke, and Jalapeño Nachos

1 large green bell pepper, chopped fine
1 tablespoon vegetable oil
2 14-ounce cans artichoke hearts,
    drained and chopped fine
2 cups mayonnaise
½ cup thinly sliced scallions
½ cup drained and chopped roasted
    red pepper or bottled pimento
1 cup freshly grated Parmesan
1½ tablespoons fresh lemon juice

4 teaspoons Worcestershire sauce
3 pickled jalapeño peppers, seeded or
    minced (wear rubber gloves while
    preparing)
1 teaspoon celery salt
1 teaspoon chopped fresh dill
1 pound crab meat, thawed and
    drained if frozen, picked over for
    bones
⅓ cup sliced almonds, toasted lightly

1. In a small cast-iron skillet, cook the bell pepper in oil over moderate heat, stirring, until it is softened. Set aside to cool.
2. In a large bowl, combine the bell pepper, artichoke hearts, mayonnaise, scallions, pimento, Parmesan, lemon juice, Worcestershire sauce, jalapeño peppers, celery salt, and dill.
3. Blend the mixture until it is combined well, and stir in the crab meat gently. Transfer the mixture to a large, buttered ovenproof casserole and sprinkle it with almonds. Cover and refrigerate until ready to serve.

4. Half an hour before serving, bake casserole in a preheated 375-degree oven for 25 to 30 minutes, or until the top is golden and the contents bubbly. Keep warm over a Sterno burner and serve with blue corn chips.

Serves 8.

Guacamole

Of all the dips that ever graced a cocktail table, this "concoction" of avocado and seasonings is the undisputed favorite. Serve it with a bowl of blue corn chips or a basket of raw vegetables and watch it disappear.

2 medium-sized avocados, ripe, but not too soft
2 tablespoons lime juice
½ cup finely chopped onion
1 tablespoon olive oil

Dash of Tabasco sauce
2 canned chili peppers, finely chopped
2 tablespoons wine vinegar
2 medium-sized tomatoes, cubed
Salt and pepper, to taste

1. Cut avocados in half, remove the pit and the peel, cut into ½-inch cubes, place in a bowl, and sprinkle with lime juice. Let marinate for 15 minutes.
2. Put the avocado cubes in container of a blender and add the chopped onion, olive oil, Tabasco, chilies, wine vinegar, and tomatoes. Blend coarse or smooth, to taste. Add salt and pepper to taste. Serve with blue corn chips.

Makes about 3 cups.

Gorgonzola-and-Walnut-Stuffed Endive Leaves

¼ pound Gorgonzola cheese
¼ pound cream cheese
¼ cup heavy cream
3 tablespoons coarsely chopped walnuts

1 teaspoon brandy
30 Belgian endive leaves (separated from 3 large Belgian endives)
30 watercress sprigs

1. Put the Gorgonzola, cream cheese, and heavy cream in a blender and mix well.

27

2. Scrape the mixture into a mixing bowl and fold in the walnuts and brandy. Chill thoroughly in the refrigerator, covered, until ready to serve.

3. Fill the lower third of each endive leaf with a heaping teaspoon of the mixture, and tuck 1 watercress sprig into the mixture on each leaf. Arrange the leaves decoratively on a platter.

Makes 30 stuffed leaves.

Dirty Shrimp and Champagne

Calvin went off to Tortola for a suntan and found there wasn't much to do except snorkel, so he chartered a boat, the *Pau Hanna*, on which I happened to be a cook. We had a serendipitous reunion, got pleasantly soused on my menu, and left the snorkling to the fish.

3 bay leaves
3 lemons, sliced
3 cloves garlic

1 cup minced scallions
3 pounds of shrimp (heads removed)

1. In a large piece of cheesecloth, tie up everything but the shrimp. Drop the seasonings into a good-sized saucepan filled with water, and boil for 15 minutes.

2. Add the shrimp to the boiling water, and continue to boil for 10 minutes.

3. Remove shrimp and chill them. Serve in a large bowl accompanied by two dipping sauces, and let each person peel, devein, and rinse his or her own in a separate jug or bowl of ice water. Provide plenty of napkins and ice cold champagne.

Serves 6 as a first course or 24 as an hors d'oeuvre.

Virgin Islands Dipping Sauce

½ cup mayonnaise
½ cup ketchup
½ cup sour cream
1 tablespoon minced onion
1 tablespoon minced fresh parsley

1 tablespoon drained sweet pickle relish
1 tablespoon Worcestershire sauce
Cayenne, to taste

1. In a serving bowl stir together the mayonnaise, ketchup, sour cream, onion, parsley, relish, Worcestershire sauce, and the cayenne until the mixture is well blended.

2. Chill the sauce, covered, for at least 1 hour or up to 24 hours.

Tomato Horseradish Dipping Sauce

1 cup ketchup
2 tablespoons fresh lemon juice
½ cup drained bottled horseradish
2 tablespoons Worcestershire sauce
¼ teaspoon dried hot red pepper flakes

¼ cup minced fresh parsley leaves
½ cup minced celery
2 scallions, minced
Parsley sprigs for garnish

1. In a serving bowl stir together the ketchup, lemon juice, horseradish, Worcestershire sauce, red pepper flakes, parsley, celery, and the scallions until the mixture is thoroughly combined.

2. Chill the sauce, covered, for at least 1 hour or up to 24 hours.

3. Garnish both sauces with parsley sprigs.

Dipping sauces serve 6 as an hors d'oeuvre.

Gravad Lax

Blue-eyed blondes aside, this is Scandinavia's second most appetizing dish in anyone's book.

7 to 8 pounds fresh salmon in one
   piece, with bones in
⅔ cup coarse salt
½ cup sugar
1 tablespoon whole white peppercorns,
   crushed

1 teaspoon whole allspice, crushed
6 tablespoons cognac
2 large bunches fresh dill

1. Buy a middle cut of salmon. Clean fish, leaving skin on. Carefully remove bones so that two big fillets remain, or let your fishmonger do the honors. Rinse in iced water and carefully dry so fish remains whole.

2. To cure, mix together salt, sugar, peppercorns, and allspice. Rub seasonings carefully into all sides of the fish. Sprinkle with cognac.

3. Wash dill and place one third of it in the bottom of a deep platter, any type but aluminum. Place one piece of salmon, skin side down, on the dill. Place another third of the dill on top of the salmon and top with the second piece of salmon, skin side up. Cover with remaining dill. Set a heavy plate or board and a 5-pound weight on the salmon. Refrigerate for 48 to 72 hours, turning the salmon and basting every 12 hours with its own juices.

4. To serve, remove fish from marinade, scrape away dill and spices, and pat dry. Slice salmon thinly on the diagonal and serve on thinly sliced Danish pumpernickel. Garnish with lemon wedges and black pepper and a dollop of dill mustard sauce.

Serves 24 as an hors d'oeuvre, and will keep about 8 days in the refrigerator, tightly wrapped in aluminum foil.

Dill Mustard Sauce

This is the classic way to sauce gravad lax, but it's a sweet and sassy dip for shrimp or crab claws, too. Serve it with buffalo grass vodka or aquavit that's been frozen into a cube of ice, and the word *skol* will have a new meaning.

9 tablespoons olive oil
3 tablespoons white vinegar
2½ tablespoons prepared mustard
¾ teaspoon salt
¼ teaspoon white pepper

¼ cup sugar
⅛ teaspoon cardamom
1 cup dairy sour cream
½ cup chopped fresh dill

1. Mix all ingredients together and blend thoroughly. The sauce should be made at least 2 hours before serving, then covered and refrigerated until ready for use.

2. Beat with a wire whisk just before serving.

Makes about 2 cups.

Chicken Liver Pâté

1 pound chicken livers
1 small onion
3/4 cup chicken stock
1 teaspoon salt
1 tablespoon Worcestershire sauce
3/4 cup butter
1/2 teaspoon paprika

1/2 teaspoon curry powder
1/4 teaspoon freshly ground black pepper
1/2 cup shelled pistachios
A splash of Burgundy wine
1 can of beef consommé (the gelatin type)

1. Simmer livers and onion in stock 10 minutes or until done; livers should still be slightly pink inside.

2. Place this mixture in the blender along with all the remaining ingredients except the pistachios, wine, and consommé. Process until very well blended and very smooth.

3. Scrape into a bowl, stir in the pistachios and a splash of Burgundy, and transfer the pâté to a 3-cup crock or terrine.

4. Smooth the top of the pâté and pour a thin layer of consommé over it. Cover, and refrigerate for at least 4 hours. Allow the pâté to stand at room temperature for 30 minutes before serving.

Serves at least 8.

Steak Tartare Dracula

1 teaspoon Dijon-style mustard
1 teaspoon fresh lemon juice
1 1/2 teaspoons Worcestershire sauce, or to taste
2 teaspoons vegetable oil
1 tablespoon bottled horseradish, or to taste
1/2 pound trimmed filet mignon or very lean trimmed sirloin, chilled well and chopped fine

2 teaspoons chopped, drained bottled capers
2 tablespoons minced scallions
Salt and freshly ground pepper
Squares of black Danish pumpernickel, each slice quartered
Fresh parsley sprigs

1. In a bowl, whisk together the mustard, lemon juice, Worcestershire sauce, oil, and horseradish.

2. Add the meat, capers, scallions, salt and freshly ground pepper to taste, and combine the mixture.

3. Mound rounded ½-teaspoons of steak tartare on each square of pumpernickel and garnish with a sprig of fresh parsley. Arrange on a platter and garnish with more parsley and fresh lemon slices.

Makes 30 bites that could satisfy even so great a connoisseur as the Count. (It gets monotonous biting into a steady diet of necks.)

Soup of the Evening

When Serendipity moved to East 60th Street in 1960, New York had two legendary cooking teachers. One, of course, was their own guru, James Beard. The other was their upstairs neighbor, Dione Lucas. She occupied what is now their parlor floor, where she conducted her Cordon Bleu Cooking School. It was thanks to Mrs. Lucas that this classic French soup became a part of the menu.

Vichyssoise
(Iced Leek and Potato Soup)

4 large potatoes, finely sliced	Salt and pepper
1 bunch leeks, finely sliced	1½ cups strong chicken or beef stock
1 small stalk celery, finely sliced	1 cup cream
1 finely sliced onion	Finely chopped fresh chives
1 cup water	Finely shredded and cooked carrots

1. Place the potatoes, leeks, celery and onion in a pan with water. Season with salt and pepper and cook very slowly until mushy.
2. Pour on the stock and bring to a boil.
3. Rub through a coarse strainer and then through a fine strainer.
4. Stir over ice until very cold.
5. Add the cream; garnish with chives and carrots. Soup is best served in bowls surrounded by crushed ice.

Serves 4.

Boston Clam Chowder

When Serendipity opened their Boston branch at Faneuil Hall, they set about to create a clam chowder that would win over the New England palate. And while there will always be clam chowder feuds and competitions, here is a worthy contender.

3 slices of bacon, diced
3 tablespoons butter
1 large onion, finely cubed
1/2 cup finely diced celery
2 1/2 cups canned minced clams
Strained clam juice plus enough water
 to equal 3 cups of liquid

2 cups raw, diced potatoes, 1/2-inch
 cubes
3 tablespoons flour
4 cups light cream
Salt and freshly ground white pepper,
 to taste

1. In a large pot on a low flame, cook the diced bacon until almost done, stirring often to prevent it from getting crisp or brown. Add the butter.

2. Add the onion and celery and sauté until tender.

3. While vegetables are cooking, place a large pot on a medium flame with the clams, clam-juice-and-water mixture, and potatoes and cook until the potatoes are tender.

4. When the onion and celery are tender, add the flour and mix well until no dry flour is left. Continue cooking on a low flame for 2 or 3 minutes more, just low enough to make the mixture golden.

5. Add the hot water and clam juice from second pot, a little at a time, mixing well after each addition until smooth and letting it simmer for 2 or 3 minutes. This will make the chowder thick and creamy.

6. When all the liquid is added, add the potatoes and clams, stirring well, and continuing to simmer for 2 or 3 minutes more.

7. Add the cream and seasonings, continuing to simmer and stir for 2 or 3 minutes more. Do not let chowder boil.

8. Serve immediately with oyster crackers.

Serves 8 die-hard New Englanders.

Red Spice Soup

5 cups tomato juice
1 cup water
2 cups canned, pureed tomatoes
1 small, finely chopped onion
1 small bunch of soup greens

In a muslin pouch, place the following
 spices and tie to close:

1 1/2 teaspoons marjoram
1/2 teaspoon anise
1/2 teaspoon fennel seeds
1/2 teaspoon sugar
1/2 teaspoon cloves
1 1/2 teaspoons salt

1. Place all liquids and the pureed tomatoes in a good-sized saucepan and heat.
2. Add the onion and soup greens, and continue simmering.
3. Place the spice bag into the soup and bring it to a boil.
4. Reduce heat to a simmer and let it cook slowly for about 5 minutes more, seasoning to taste and stirring. Remove spice bag and serve.

Serves 6 to 8.

Autumn Vegetable Soup

A brimming bowl of this hearty country soup on a blustery night needs only some crusty bread and butter, a crisp salad, and warm Big Apple pie to take away the chill. Make it the day before. Overnight refrigeration and reheating only intensifies the flavor.

4 tablespoons butter
1 cup finely diced yellow onion
2 leeks
1/2 cup chopped celery tops
1/2 cup chopped Italian parsley
4 carrots, peeled and sliced
4 parsnips, peeled and sliced
1 1/2 turnips, peeled, quartered and sliced

8 cups chicken stock, skimmed
1/2 teaspoon salt
1/2 teaspoon freshly ground black pepper
1 teaspoon chopped fresh basil
1/2 teaspoon chopped fresh rosemary
1 1/2 cups navy beans, cooked
4 or 5 cooked sausages, sliced

1. In a large pot, melt the butter, then add the onion and cook until soft.
2. Add chopped leeks, celery tops, and parsley and cook 2 minutes more. Add carrots, parsnips, and turnips.
3. Cook until vegetables are soft, then add soup stock.
4. Add spices and simmer for 15 minutes more, then skim off most of the spices.
5. Add sausages and navy beans, simmer for another 5 minutes or so. Taste, correct seasoning, and serve immediately.

Serves up to 10 for lunch, 8 for supper.

Kentucky Corn Chowder

1 can of corn kernels, drained
2 onions, sliced
4 tablespoons butter
4 cups of milk

4 slices of bacon, fried and cut in
   small pieces
Salt, pepper to taste
Chopped parsley
4 tablespoons bourbon

1. Sauté onions in 1 tablespoon butter.
2. Mix corn, sautéed onions, and milk in blender.
3. Transfer mixture to good-sized saucepan. Add all ingredients (including remaining 3 tablespoons butter) except the bourbon and heat thoroughly, stirring constantly.
4. Put one tablespoon of bourbon in four prewarmed soup cups. Pour in the chowder, stir, and serve as the heartiest course in the meal.

Serves 4.

Gazpacho

2 cucumbers, finely chopped
1 sweet onion, finely chopped
1 green pepper, seeded and chopped
4 large ripe tomatoes, chopped
1 teaspoon red pimento
1 or 2 cloves of garlic, finely minced

1 cup tomato juice
2 tablespoons red wine vinegar
1/8 teaspoon cayenne pepper
Freshly ground black pepper
1 teaspoon chopped fresh dill

Garnishes:

1 cucumber, seeded, peeled, and diced
1 green or red pepper, seeded and diced
Finely chopped chives, 4–6 teaspoons
   to taste

1/2 cup sour cream
1 cup garlic croutons

1. In a food processor fitted with a steel blade, puree the vegetables and garlic bit by bit, blending in the tomato juice and vinegar to prevent clogging.

Do not completely liquify. Gazpacho should be thick and a little crunchy.

2. Stir in the cayenne, salt and pepper to taste, and add the dill. Cover and refrigerate for a good 4 to 6 hours.

3. Garnish just before serving with cucumber, pepper, and chives. A dollop of sour cream and garlic croutons make this spicy "liquid salad" even zestier.

Serves 6.

Onion Soup Chef Arnold

4 tablespoons butter
6 medium-sized onions, finely sliced
1 clove garlic, mashed to a paste
Salt and pepper
2 quarts soup stock or bouillon, prepared according to directions on the can

1 dash Worcestershire sauce
1 bay leaf
1/4 teaspoon dried thyme
5 ounces Calvados
6 slices French bread
1 cup grated Gruyère cheese

1. Melt the butter in a Dutch oven or marmite. Add the onions, garlic, salt and pepper, and sauté slowly to a very dark brown over a low fire for roughly 30 minutes.

2. Add the soup stock, Worcestershire sauce, bay leaf, and thyme and stir well. Bring the mixture slowly to a boil. Add the Calvados and simmer for 25 minutes.

3. Pour into individual marmites. Add a slice of bread to each. Cover surface with grated cheese and brown quickly under the broiler. Serve piping hot.

Serves 6.

Champagne Onion Soup

Some people don't wake up till after the final curtain, when this late supper eye-opener is on the menu. Follow it with cold meat and a salad, and hold for applause.

7 onions
4 tablespoons butter
2 tablespoons flour
2 quarts water
1 pint stock
2 glasses champagne

Salt and pepper, to taste
6 slices French bread, or more, to
   taste
1/4–1/2 pound grated Gruyère, or to
   taste

1. Slice 5 onions and brown well in 2 tablespoons butter. Add the flour and stir until the mixture thickens.

2. Transfer the mixture to a large saucepan. Add the water, stock, and champagne. Cook slowly for 30 minutes, adding salt and pepper to taste.

3. Meanwhile, cover the bottom of a deep casserole with slices of French bread; sprinkle generously with grated Gruyère cheese until the casserole is half filled. Slice remaining 2 onions and, in another skillet, cook additional slices of onion in butter, but do not brown them.

4. Strain the soup, add the freshly cooked onions, and all at once pour over bread and cheese in casserole. Cover the top with additional slices of bread and Gruyère and bake in the oven for 15 minutes at 350 degrees.

Serves 6.

Jellied Borscht Silvermine

4 cups strong beef stock
1 bunch raw beets, grated
1/2 cup red wine
2 tablespoons tomato paste
2 bay leaves
3 stiffly beaten egg whites
4 tablespoons (2 envelopes) unflavored
   gelatin

Grated rind of one lemon
Salt
Cayenne pepper
5 tablespoons sour cream
Black caviar

1. Pour the stock into a tin-lined copper pan or heavy aluminum stewpot. Add the beets, wine, tomato paste, bay leaves, and egg whites. Add the gelatin and heat over the fire until the borscht comes to a boil. Put it aside and allow it to cool.

2. Pour through a fine damp cloth, or a sieve; then beat the gelatin into the clear borscht.

3. Ladle into individual soup bowls and refrigerate until firm. Add the grated lemon rind, salt, and pepper to the sour cream and garnish with a dollop each of cream and caviar. Serve with thin slices of dark pumpernickel with sweet butter.

Serves 6.

Crepes, Pancakes, Waffles and Fritters

(*continued from page 22*)

had a narrow escape, his wife having persuaded him to keep his pants on and go around the corner to Serendipity instead. She had been trying to wean him away from his nightly Scotch-and-sodas and she succeeded. He never set foot in La Rue again. Shocked into sobriety, his customary "nightcap" was now a cinnamon-spiked cappuccino. We have it on good authority that he refuses to wear underwear to this day, and that he still calls his nightly Serendipity cappuccino, "One for the road."

All the night owls who roosted in Serendipity were not necessarily teeto-talers. One of them, referred to here as Madame X, was a notorious Park Avenue socialite who was never entirely sober, and always a little in love. Her passion was for very young men. She never left home without refilling the silver sherry flask she kept in her Hermès handbag. Tonight it was empty. As she tottered down the rickety cast-iron steps, she wailed, "That apricot smush or I'll die." There was a brief pause while the owners considered this latest test of their legendary Southern hospitality. "Never say no," was tattooed on their chests. "We're just out of apricots," they replied. "Come back tomorrow." In less time than it took Madame X to get smashed, she had her apricot smush, frozen, under a mountain of whipped cream and nonpareils. Apprehensive in her sobriety, she whimpered, "I'll die of it." "If you do, Madame," came Patch's soothing reply, "you'll die magnificently."

After a couple of spoonfuls, she bolted for the ladies room, latched the door, and commenced to sob. Her weeping and wailing shook the house and Patch, concerned, tapped gently at the door and offered assistance. She threw open the door, flung her arms around his neck and wept, "You look just like him." She was mourning her last lost love, a twenty-year-old hairdresser who had escaped her clutches with difficulty, despite her bribes of a generous weekly allowance, the use of her limousine, and an unlimited charge account at the Brothers Brooks. Poor Patch extricated himself from her iron grip, slid her into her sable and out the door, hailing a cab. When he returned, he found a fifty dollar "gratuity" on her table.

On the night of a record blizzard, when the world was housebound, the Serendips were debating whether they should call it a night and go home early. Suddenly, two orphans of the storm appeared on their doorstep, encased in snow-covered fur like a couple of characters in *Northwest Passage*, illustrated by Edward Gorey.

Ursule Molinero was a published poet, a rich urchin in floor-length fox. She was the mysterious lady in black down to her onyx-lacqured fingertips. Her raccoon-muffled companion was Venable Hendron, an aspiring playwright just out of Harvard. They were astonished to have stumbled on what appeared to be the cave of Ali Baba and the Forty Thieves. Or does frostbite bring on a mirage?

As in the days when mail couriers took their duties to heart, neither snow nor sleet nor dead of night could keep dauntless Ursule and Venable from Serendipity's door. Venable remembers a party where "a Julliard student, wearing a laurel wreath, played a cello. This was a bit of Victorian nonsense of the most exquisite sort. It was the beginning of an all-white aestheticism. Eclectic clutter, none of it costing too much, gave people permission to do the same. Café life was just reaching America, just as New York art was displacing Paris, London, and Rome. Now there was a cheap way to acquire style. It didn't have to be Louis XIV. It needn't be purchased at Sotheby's. Taste and flair were enough."

Serendipity began to combine clashing, unmatched colors and made them as appealing as a canvas by Matisse. It became a little theater of the absurd in which Patch played gentleman of the plantation, Calvin burlesqued that gentleman, and Stephen, in charge of costumes, called the dress code of the '50s to task, breaking rules left and right. Together, they created an unrepressed haven in a very restrictive time.

Philippe Julienne's book, *Decadence in New York*, was published as the fifties were drawing to a close. In it, Serendipity was cited as the setting for the latest lost generation, the naive, drugless depravity of the 1950s.

On the final Friday the thirteenth of the fifties, and on thirteen Friday the thirteenths thereafter, Molinero read the palms of the three Princes of Serendip and gave them her predictions for the coming year. They never made a move without consulting her. They had long outgrown their impossibly tiny *boite de sardines*. Neighbors complained about their ever-lengthening waiting line. Stephen discovered that the main floor of a charming brownstone at 225 East 60th Street was in search of a tenant. It seemed a setting made in heaven for them. But it was not until Molinero studied their numerology charts, and assured them that they were in harmonious vibration with the numbers of this new location that they were totally convinced.

Even the invisible parrot (*continued on page 53*)

Crepes

1 tablespoon butter	1/2 teaspoon salt
2 eggs	1 teaspoon double-acting baking pow-
2/3 cup milk	der
1/3 cup water	3/4 teaspoon orange rind, grated fine
3/4 cup all-purpose flour, sifted	1 teaspoon brandy

1. Melt the butter in a small pan and set aside.
2. Crack the eggs in a mixing bowl, add the milk and water, and beat with a wire whisk.
3. Resift the flour with salt and baking powder in another bowl. Add the egg and milk mixture slowly to the flour mixture and begin whisking in the center, working your way out as the mixture thickens.
4. Add the melted butter, incorporating it well. Next add the orange rind and brandy. If there are lumps, ignore them. They will take care of themselves.
5. Heat a 5-inch skillet. Grease it lightly with a few drops of oil. Add a small quantity of batter. Tip the skillet and let the batter spread over the entire bottom. Cook the crepe over moderate heat. When it is brown underneath, reverse it and brown the other side. Remove to a platter. Continue cooking the rest of the crepes in like manner, using a few drops of oil for each crepe.

Makes about 14 to 16 5-inch crepes.

Creamed Chicken Crepes

1. Prepare Creamed Chicken for Waffles (page 50).
2. Place a generous portion of Creamed Chicken on each crepe.
3. Roll or fold crepe over the filling and spoon some of the White Sauce over the top. Garnish with parsley and watercress and serve.

White Sauce for Creamed Chicken Crepes

1 cup chicken stock, skimmed
1/2 cup milk
1/3 cup heavy cream
2 tablespoons butter

1 tablespoon chicken fat
1 1/2 to 2 tablespoons flour
Freshly ground black pepper and salt,
   to taste

1. In a small saucepan, combine stock, milk, and cream, reserving half the stock. Stir and heat, over a low flame.

2. In a larger saucepan, melt together the butter and fat. Add flour and reserved stock and whisk thoroughly.

3. Gradually add the first mixture to the second, continuing to whisk over a low heat. Whisking will keep sauce from sticking to the sides of the pan. Mixture will start to thicken. Add a small amount of flour while whisking. Sauce should be the consistency of honey. Season to taste.

Makes about 2½ cups.

Chili with Cheese Crepes

1. See Chili (page 83).

2. Place a good portion of chili on the center of the crepe.

3. Roll or fold crepe over the chili and sprinkle the top with grated cheddar cheese. Pass it briefly under the broiler to melt. Garnish with parsley and chopped purple onions and serve.

Spinach Crepes

1 package frozen spinach
1 clove garlic, chopped fine
Juice of 1/2 lemon
2 tablespoons olive oil

2 tablespoons melted butter
6 crepes
Hollandaise Sauce (see A White
   Christmas Dinner, page 197)

1. Cut the frozen spinach block into small pieces with a heavy knife. Place in a heavy saucepan, covered, over a low heat to thaw. When thawed, remove from heat, drain in a sieve or colander, and chop very fine.

2. Blend spinach with chopped garlic and lemon juice and beat in the olive oil. Drain again.

3. Place a good portion of spinach on each of 6 crepes. Roll, brush with melted butter, and heat in a 400-degree oven for a few minutes.

4. Serve with a slice of ham and dress with a generous helping of Hollandaise sauce.

Serves 6.

Puff Pancakes

1½ cups flour, sifted before measuring
3 tablespoons sugar
1 teaspoon salt
4 eggs, separated

1 cup milk
½ teaspoon vanilla extract
3 tablespoons butter, melted

1. Resift the flour with sugar and salt and place in a blender.
2. In a separate bowl, beat the egg yolks until they are light and thick, add the milk and vanilla, and mix them. Add them gradually to the flour in the blender while it is on low speed.
3. Continue to mix on low speed until smooth. Meanwhile, in a separate bowl, beat the egg whites until they are stiff, and add them to the batter. Mix only briefly, then stop.
4. Add 3 tablespoons melted butter, and blend in quickly. Test the griddle, which has been heating, by letting a few drops of cold water fall on it. If they bounce and sputter, the griddle is ready.
5. Let batter pour from the tip of the spoon for a well-rounded cake. Let bake for 2 or 3 minutes. When bubbles appear on top of the cakes, they are ready to turn. Lift with a spatula to see how well they have browned. Turn only once, baking the second side half as long as the first.

Makes 14 4-inch cakes.

Whole Wheat Pancakes

1. Prepare them as in Puff Pancakes, substituting

¾ cup cake flour   ¾ cup whole wheat flour

for the 1½ cups flour in Puff Pancakes (page 46).

Serve either recipe with blueberry sauce.

Blueberry Sauce

1 cup sugar   1½ cups fresh or thawed frozen blue-
2 tablespoons cornstarch   berries
½ cup water   1½ teaspoons lemon juice

1. Combine sugar and cornstarch in a saucepan, mixing the two together to blend thoroughly, making sure the cornstarch is not lumpy. Stir in the water.
2. Drain blueberries. If frozen are used, be sure there is no excess liquid. Stir the berries into the sugar mixture along with the lemon juice.
3. Cook over medium heat, stirring constantly until mixture boils and thickens.
4. Remove from the heat and allow to cool at room temperature. Cover and store in the refrigerator until ready to use over pancakes, waffles, or ice cream.

Makes about 3 cups.

Chocolate Pancakes

4 eggs, separated   ¼ cup sifted flour
¼ cup water   ¼ cup instant chocolate mix

1. Heat pancake griddle to 350 degrees. Beat the egg yolks until they are light and thick.

2. Beat in the water, flour, and chocolate mix, blending well.

3. In a separate bowl, beat the egg whites until they hold glossy peaks. Add to the egg yolk mixture.

4. Brush the griddle with sweet butter. Drop chocolate mixture by table-spoonsfuls. Fry until delicately brown on both sides, turning only once. Serve with sour cherry preserves.

Makes 6 portions of 2 pancakes each.

Wild Rice Griddle Cakes

1/4 cup cornmeal	6 tablespoons milk
3/4 teaspoon sugar	1/2 cup sifted flour
3/4 teaspoon salt	1 1/2 teaspoons baking powder
1/4 teaspoon pepper	1 small egg, beaten
1/2 cup boiling water	1 cup cooked wild rice

1. Place cornmeal, sugar, salt, and pepper in a bowl. Add boiling water and stir until well mixed.

2. Add milk, sift in flour and baking powder, and stir.

3. Beat in egg, then fold in wild rice.

4. Drop 1 tablespoon of batter at a time onto a lightly greased hot griddle or skillet. Cook cakes over medium-high heat until bubbles form on tops, and edges become a bit dry. Flip cakes and cook until done.

Makes 14 4-inch cakes.

Bacon and Sliced Apple Pancake

Prepare sliced, cored apple wedges, approximately 1/4-inch thick.   *Bacon, sliced thick, and blanched*

1. Pour thin pancake batter (dilute it with a little water) into a large, buttered skillet. Arrange apple wedges and bacon on top of batter.

2. Brown the bottom nicely over a moderate heat.

3. Flip and brown the reverse side.

4. Serve flat or rolled with maple syrup, powdered sugar, or jam.

Potato Pancake

Basic pancake batter   *Red caviar*
1½ cups grated potato   *Sour cream*
2 tablespoons butter

1. To pancake batter, add grated potato.
2. Heat a heavy 6-inch skillet, and melt the butter in the bottom. Pour enough pancake mixture in to completely cover the bottom of the skillet.
3. Brown it on one side, flip pancake, and brown the reverse side as well.
4. Roll the pancake, top with sour cream and red caviar, and serve.

Waffles with Creamed Chicken

4 cups flour   *6 eggs, separated*
1 teaspoon salt   *⅔ cup melted butter*
2 tablespoons sugar   *2½ cups milk*
4 teaspoons baking powder

1. Sift together the first four dry ingredients.
2. In a separate bowl, combine the 6 egg yolks, ⅔ cup of melted butter, and 2½ cups of milk. Whisk them all together, blending well.
3. Whisk together the flour and egg mixtures, beating thoroughly.
4. In a clean bowl, beat the egg whites until stiff and fold them into the batter. Do not mix too thoroughly. Batter will keep up to three days if covered and refrigerated.
5. Heat the waffle iron until the indicator shows it is ready to use. If it has been properly conditioned, it will need no greasing. Pour batter in a pitcher and cover the grid surface two-thirds full. Close lid and wait 4 minutes. When waffle is ready, steam will stop emerging from crack in waffle iron. (If you try to lift the lid and it sticks, the waffle is not quite done. Give it a minute and try again.)

Makes 12 waffles.

Creamed Chicken for Waffles

1/2 cup chicken fat
1/4 pound of butter, melted
1 cup plus 2 tablespoons flour
6 cups chicken stock
3 chicken bouillon cubes

1/2 quart of milk
1 can evaporated milk
4 cups diced chicken, both light and
   dark meat
Salt and pepper, to taste

1. Over a low flame, cook chicken fat, butter, and flour in a large saucepan. Simmer slowly, stirring, until well blended. Slowly add chicken stock, bouillon cubes, and both the milk and the evaporated milk. Add the chicken, stir well, and simmer for 5 to 10 minutes, heating thoroughly. Season with salt and pepper. Serve the creamed chicken over the waffles.

Serves 12. To serve 6, store half the sauce in the refrigerator, covered, and add only 2 cups of diced chicken.

Moonshine Apple Fritters

1 egg
1 tablespoon sugar
1 teaspoon salt
1 cup milk
2/3 cup flour (or enough to make a
   heavy batter)

1 teaspoon double-acting baking
   powder
1 tablespoon rum
4 to 6 apples, cored
Shortening for frying

1. Beat the egg well in a bowl with a wire whisk.
2. Add sugar, salt, and milk alternately with flour (in which baking powder has been sifted). Mix thoroughly to make a smooth batter, blending in the rum as you whisk.
3. Cut each apple in 4 or more slices across, according to your preference, and dip them in batter.
4. Put the shortening at least one inch deep in a heavy, black cast-iron skillet. Fry the apple slices until the batter turns golden brown on one side, then reverse and fry to golden brown on the other side.

Serves 8.

Ftatateeta's Toast

Pinch of ground cinnamon
Pinch of ground nutmeg
Pinch of finely grated orange rind
1 tablespoon brandy
⅔ cup milk
2 eggs

8 slices of white bread, the crusts
trimmed to form a uniform edge
1 package Philadelphia Cream Cheese
(large)
Rhubarb and ginger jam

1. Combine the spices, orange rind, and brandy in a mixing bowl and beat with a wire whisk.

2. Add milk and continue whisking.

3. Crack eggs in a separate bowl and whisk until frothy. Add eggs to the mixture and blend well.

4. Dip all 8 slices of bread in this mixture and brown them on one side, on a hot, well-buttered griddle. Reverse, cover 4 sides with generous slices of cream cheese. Cover cream cheese with remaining 4 slices, browned side down. When bottom 4 sides have browned on the griddle, transfer to broiler to brown top sides.

5. Cut each sandwich in half, 4 halves to a portion, and place a dollop of rhubarb and ginger jam on each half.

Ftatateeta was Cleopatra's handmaiden. You might need a handmaiden to execute this toast. You're worth it.

Serves 2 if you're off Weight Watchers™.

(*continued from page 43*)
on Molinaro's shoulder squawked, "Polly wanna move. Polly wanna move." So they did.

John F. Kennedy's dream of Camelot ushered in the happy-ever-after climate of the 1960s and Serendipity's move to 60th Street. The three princes took command of their new realm with a magic blend of irreverence and freewheeling imagination. They were so attractive, so cocky, so clever, so brimming with energy. Not since Lewis Carroll had there been such a spot for the pleasantly unexpected.

By their oddball assortment of employees, they were looked upon as princes of a don't-let's-count-calories domain that, for sheer comedy, rivaled the mythical kingdom of Gilbert and Sullivan's *Mikado*. They were generous, even democratic, but they remained Mikados with a Lord High Executioner waiting to lop off the heads of any disloyal, incompetent, or light-fingered subject. Waiters were right out of Central Casting, chosen not only for their good looks, charm, and showmanship, but also for their astrological compatibility with their lordships. Hence, Sylvester Stallone was refused a job because of a lightly askew birth sign, and had to console himself by playing Rocky I, II, III, and IV in Hollywood.

Former Serendipity waiters tend to shine in their own constellations. One is now a chief creative honcho on a prestigious magazine; another is a porn star in such films as *Boys in the Sand*; a third, playing the lead in a made-for-TV film, recalled, in an interview, the chauffeured limousines lining up to pick up Frozen Hot Chocolates when he was a Serendipity waiter. James La Force, now a public relations executive with Eleanor Lambert, was fired and rehired three times, each time by a new manager whose predecessor had been fired. A quick study with a guileless choirboy face, all James needed was a new haircut to get his job back. He found a home at last in the spin-on-a-dime world of PR.

The management was justly proud of its unspoken law, the Napoleonic code. Once someone was seated and served, it was a mortal sin to hover and hint for him to leave. Some guests took advantage and overstayed their welcome. A special announcement became necessary: "Hail! Minimum charge, $1" appeared on each table. "Big Bird" Toomey, six-feet-seven-inches of unflappability, remembers the night his patience was pushed to the breaking point. The entire staff had gone home. A couple of old biddies sat glued to their table, deep in conversation, oblivious of the empty restaurant around them. He had already missed his midnight subway connection. Desperate to get the last train home, he went into the Gents room, stripped down to his shoes and socks, and came out in (*continued on page 70*)

Open-Face Vegetable Sandwich

For years a favorite, its secret is in the pecan-miso spread (below), which goes on the homemade whole wheat bread. But we'll come to that in good time.

2 slices whole wheat bread
2 or 3 tablespoons Serendip Pecan
  Butter (below)
Crisp slices of Granny Smith apple
Sliced fresh, white, unblemished mushrooms

Sliced green bell peppers
Sliced cucumber (if you want to be
  very la-di-da, you can gouge out the
  seeded core)
Fistful of alfalfa sprouts

1. Spread the pecan butter lavishly on thickly sliced whole wheat or whole grain bread, remembering that we're after health here.
2. Pile on the apple slices and veggies in the order given and you'll feel very virtuous. You may want to add a little Lemon-Lime or Curry-Chutney Dressing (page 76) to this mountain of nutrition.

Serendip Pecan Butter

1 cup chopped pecans
*1 tablespoon miso paste**
3 tablespoons honey

⅓ cup plain yogurt
1 teaspoon soy sauce

1. In a bowl, whisk all ingredients together until you have a smooth, spreadable, mouth-watering paste. If it seems a little too thick, add a touch more honey or yogurt.

Makes about 1½ cups.

* Available in Asian food stores.

Ricotta Cheese Sandwich

The magic here is in the lemon curd, a staple of British teas that is customarily served with scones and sweet buns. It is pleasantly unexpected in the vegetable kingdom. But we never said vegetables had to be boring.

*2 hefty slices of homemade 7-grain
   bread*
*2 healthy smears of lemon curd dress-
   ing (below)*
Crisp slices of Granny Smith apple
*Sliced fresh, white, unblemished mush-
   rooms*

Sliced green bell peppers
Sliced, de-seeded cucumber
A clump of alfalfa sprouts
A generous mound of ricotta cheese

1. Butter your bread thickly with lemon curd.
2. Layer on the apple slices and vegetables, in the order given, and "varnish" the sprouts with more lemon curd.
3. Cover this tower of health with a nice, thick helping of ricotta cheese. Pass the creation under the broiler until the ricotta melts and is slightly golden, and dig in.

Lemon Curd

*1 cup fresh lemon juice (4 to 6 lem-
   ons)*
¼ cup finely shredded lemon peel

1¼ cups sugar
6 tablespoons butter
3 eggs, lightly beaten

1. In a medium saucepan, combine the lemon juice, lemon peel, and sugar. Bring to a boil and simmer for 5 minutes. Add the butter and stir until it has melted. Remove the mixture from the heat and cool to room temperature.
2. Beat the eggs into the lemon-sugar mixture until well and truly whisked and place over low heat. Bring to just below the simmering point and cook, stirring constantly, for 7 to 10 minutes, or until the mixture thickens and coats the spoon.
3. Remove from heat and pour into one 2-cup or two 1-cup sterilized

French *confiture* (jam) jars. Cool, cover, and refrigerate. Cut squares of Pierre Deux Provençal or other decorative prints with pinking shears, tie with ribbon and make a gift of this serendipitous conserve, along with the recipe.

Makes 1½ cups, exhilarating on scones, biscuits and breakfast toast.*

The Ultimate B.L.T.

The surprise element in this composition is challah bread with its rich, briochelike flavor.

2 slices challah bread
2 tablespoons mayonnaise
Few leaves of crisp Bibb lettuce
A few slices of beefsteak tomato

5 slices bacon, as lean and thick as
  you can get it, and not too overfried
  (halfway done should do it)

1. Spread challah slices generously with mayonnaise.
2. Load on the lettuce, the tomato, and the bacon last.
3. Cover with second slice of challah and cut sandwich in half. Serve with a glass of ice cold milk to a growing boy.

Chicken Salad Sandwich

2 slices Irish soda bread, toasted
2 leaves Bibb lettuce
8 ounces Chicken Julia (page 71)

Few sprigs watercress, cucumber slices,
  black olives for garnish

1. Butter both slices of toasted soda bread.
2. Cover 1 slice with lettuce, Chicken Julia, and top with second slice of toast.
3. Slice sandwich in half and garnish with watercress, cucumber, and olives.

---

* Share the find at Christmas. Quadruple the recipe and pack into French confiture jars (set of 6 with covers available at Williams Sonoma, 20 East 60th Street, New York City). Cover tops in squares of Pierre Deux Provençal cotton, 870 Madison Ave., New York, and tie with a bright ribbon.

Shrimp Salad Sandwich

2 slices Irish soda bread, toasted
2 leaves Bibb lettuce
8 ounces shrimp salad

Watercress, cucumber slices, black olives for garnish

1. Butter both slices of toasted soda bread.
2. Cover 1 slice with lettuce, shrimp salad, and top with second slice of toast.
3. Cut sandwich in half, garnish and serve.

Shrimp Salad

10 ounces cooked shrimp, peeled, cleaned, and coarsely chopped
1 hard-boiled egg
5 dashes of Tabasco

6 ounces of finely minced celery
Juice of a fresh lemon
Enough mayonnaise to bind the shrimp, egg, and celery.

1. Mix all ingredients and serve.

Serves 2.

Virginia Slim Open

2 slices of crusty, homemade whole wheat bread
Butter

6 ounces of turkey breast, sliced thin
6 stalks white asparagus, steamed
2 hearty slices of Jarlsberg cheese

1. Spread both slices of bread with butter.
2. Build an open-face sandwich: layer 1, turkey across both slices; layer 2, asparagus, across both slices; layer 3, 1 slab Jarlsberg on each slice.
3. Pass under the broiler, melt and brown slightly, and serve

High Heel Pump

2 slices raisin pumpernickel
2 or 3 tablespoons Russian dressing
Few leaves of Bibb lettuce

Beefsteak tomato slices
¼ pound finely sliced prosciutto
¼ pound wedge of brie

1. Spread 2 slices of raisin pumpernickel with Russian dressing.
2. On one slice, place the lettuce leaves, tomato slices, ham, and brie.
3. Cover with second slice, cut sandwich in half and serve.

Russian Dressing

¼ cup chili sauce

¼ cup mayonnaise

1. Mix both ingredients together thoroughly and spread on bread.

Makes ½ cup.

Young Chicken Sandwich

6 ounces skinless, boneless chicken
  breasts, precooked
4 tablespoons butter
3 tablespoons sliced almonds

Salt
2 slices Irish soda bread, toasted
3 sprigs watercress, cucumber slices,
  black olives for garnish

1. Sauté chicken breasts in 2 tablespoons butter on high flame in heavy skillet until they are crisp and brown on both sides.
2. Meanwhile, toast almonds in pan with salt and 1 tablespoon butter, stirring to keep them from burning.
3. To build sandwich: With remaining 1 tablespoon butter, butter toast on one side only. Cover one piece of toast with chicken; top with toasted almonds. Cover with second slice of toast, buttered side down.
4. Slice sandwich in half and garnish.

Pimento Cheese Sandwich

½ cup cheddar cheese, grated
1 whole pimento, chopped fine
5 dashes Tabasco sauce
1 tablespoon mayonnaise

2 hefty slices of crusty Italian whole
  wheat bread, lightly toasted
3 pickle slices

1. Blend the cheese, pimento, Tabasco, and mayonnaise to make a smooth paste.
2. Spread the mixture on one slice of bread.
3. Place 3 pickle slices on mixture and close sandwich.

You are now in the deep south of a little boy's lunch box.

Foot-Long Hot Dog

1 hot dog roll
1 tablespoon butter
1 foot-long hot dog
1 ladle chili

2 tablespoons minced purple onion
Minced parsley
2 tablespoons sour cream
1 ladle coleslaw

1. Split hot dog roll in half and butter each half. Grill until brown and crisp.
2. At the same time, grill a foot-long hot dog until thoroughly hot and juicy.
3. On a celery dish, place the hot dog on top of the open grilled roll. Top with one ladle of chili (see recipe in Casseroles, page 83), sprinkle with minced purple onion, parsley, and sour cream. Serve with a ladle of coleslaw (page 109).

The Beardburger

Once you've tasted Serendipity hamburgers, you'll never go back to McDonald's. The incomparable James Beard invented them exclusively for Serendipity, and now you can share the secret.

1 bunch of parsley	*½ teaspoon pepper*
1 large onion	*2 pounds lean ground sirloin*
3 eggs	*1 cup breadcrumbs*
½ teaspoon salt	*3 teaspoons butter*

1. Mix the first 5 ingredients in a blender until they become liquefied. Add the ground sirloin and continue mixing until the ingredients are thoroughly integrated.

2. Divide into four 8-ounce balls and flatten each into 1-inch thick patties. Dip both sides of each burger in breadcrumbs.

3. Heat a black cast-iron skillet and melt the butter. Pan broil the burger to the degree desired, rare, medium, or well-done. Have it as is or top with your heart's desire: chili (page 83); curried mushrooms (page 66); Deviled Sauce (page 107); fonduta, Jarlsberg, or cheddar cheese; bacon; sour-cream-cucumber-and-caviar; au poivre sauce (page 105); or Marilyn Monroe (page 144).

Serves 4.

Kiss-Me-Not Below the Mason-Dixon Line

When Calvin Holt was a barefoot five-year-old, pulling his little red wagon around his grandpa's farm, this was his favorite sandwich.

2–3 tablespoons chunky peanut butter	*3 or 4 slices Irish bacon, grilled*
or Serendip Pecan Butter	*2 slices Vidalia onion*
2 slices white bread	*1 tablespoon mayonnaise*

1. Spread peanut or pecan butter on one slice of bread.
2. Cover with bacon slices.
3. Cover with onion.
4. Spread second slice with mayonnaise and close sandwich.

It may not be purist, but a generous sprinkling of finely chopped parsley on the onion could make this a Kiss-Me-Above the Mason-Dixon Line Sandwich. Try it.

Grilled Antipasto

2 slices challah bread
¼ pound thinly sliced prosciutto
½ ounce Jarlsberg cheese, sliced

½ ounce mozzarella cheese, sliced
2 tablespoons marinated antipasto
salad

1. Toast the challah on one side.
2. On the toasted side of one slice, place prosciutto, cheeses, and antipasto salad.
3. Close sandwich with toasted side of bread down. Grill until cheese is melted and toast is brown.

Serves 1.

Bathed Bread

1 long loaf French bread, sliced in
half, lengthwise
4 tablespoons olive oil
1 tomato, sliced thin
1 green pepper, sliced in strips

1 small purple onion, sliced thin
1 small can anchovy filets
1 3-ounce can white tunafish in oil
6 or 8 pitted Spanish olives, chopped
Red wine vinegar and extra olive oil

1. Generously brush each inside half of the bread with the olive oil.
2. Arrange overlapping layers of tomatoes, green pepper strips, onion rings, anchovies, tunafish, and Spanish olives.
3. Dribble vinegar and oil over the layers, cover with top half of loaf, and, with hands, firmly press two halves together. Allow to set. Slice loaf in sandwich-sized portions.

Serves 2.

Tea Sandwiches

2½-pound round loaf of white bread, homemade (recipe under Bread, page 122)

Smoked Salmon and Cucumber Sandwiches

¼ pound cream cheese	*1 tablespoon minced onion*
¼ stick butter, softened	*Salt and pepper*
2 tablespoons fresh dill, finely chopped	*1 cucumber*
2 teaspoons fresh lemon juice	*¼ pound thinly sliced smoked salmon*

1. In a small bowl, cream the cream cheese with the butter and add dill, lemon juice, minced onion, and salt and pepper to taste.

2. Peel the cucumber and cut it in half lengthwise. Remove all seeds and grate it into the cream cheese mixture. Mix thoroughly so it is evenly distributed.

3. Spread this mixture evenly on 8 slices of bread from which the crust has been trimmed. On 4 of these slices, arrange smoked salmon in one layer. Press remaining 4 slices, cheese-spread side down, on top of the salmon and cut each into 4 wedges.

Makes 16 tea sandwiches.

Curried Chicken Sandwiches

2 teaspoons curry powder	*1 cup minced cooked chicken*
2 teaspoons vegetable oil	*½ cup chopped pecans*
¼ teaspoon firmly packed light brown sugar	*½ cup plus 1 tablespoon mayonnaise*
2 teaspoons raspberry vinegar	*3 tablespoons minced fresh coriander*
1 teaspoon grated onion	*Salt and pepper*
1 hard-boiled egg, finely chopped	*8 slices of bread*

1. In a small skillet, cook the curry powder in the oil over moderately low heat, stirring for 3 minutes. Stir in the brown sugar and vinegar and let mixture cool.

2. In a bowl, toss together the onion, egg, chicken, pecans, curry mixture,

½ cup of the mayonnaise, 1 tablespoon of the coriander, and salt and pepper to taste.

3. Spread curried chicken on 4 slices of bread, trimmed. Press 4 slices of trimmed bread on top of chicken and cut each into 4 wedges. Spread 1 tablespoon of mayonnaise on outside edges and dip them in remaining coriander.

Makes 16 tea sandwiches.

Omelettes

The Basic Omelette

James Beard's lessons in omelette-making have been passed on to successive Serendipity chefs who, for thirty-six years, have been turning out the most flawless French omelettes in town. This is how the mystery unfolds, or rather, folds.

First, you must have the ideal omelette pan: heavy cast aluminum, approximately 8 inches in diameter. It must be used for omelettes and crepes exclusively, and never washed with soap and water, just wiped clean with a paper towel and salt. Its sides must be sloping, its handle must be longish for easy maneuvering. And it must be seasoned, when new, by heating a tablespoon of butter in it slowly, adding ½ teaspoon of salt, and rubbing it well with a paper towel.

¼ teaspoon salt
2 tablespoons water (or beer)
¼ teaspoon Tabasco (omit for sweet
 omelettes)

3 fresh eggs at room temperature
1 tablespoon butter

1. In a cup, dissolve salt in water (or beer) and Tabasco. Break eggs in a bowl and beat with a wire whisk just enough to mix them (overbeating makes them watery and tough). The eggs should look stringy and make a sticky thread when you lift up the whisk. Add first mixture and stir until just mixed.

2. Place pan over medium heat until drops of water, sprinkled on pan, bounce, jump, and immediately disappear. If pan smokes, it is too hot. Remove from heat for a few seconds.

3. Put 1 tablespoon butter in pan, and coat sides and bottom well. Quickly pour in the eggs. Working fast, make quick circular motions with a dinner fork on the bottom of the pan while shaking pan back and forth to raise layers of fluffiness.

4. After 8 or 10 circular motions, spread eggs evenly over bottom of pan. Pause a second or two until eggs barely set and look glistening. The omelette is ready to be rolled if the outer edges can be lifted easily with a fork away from the pan.

5. Tilt pan 45 degrees, and with a fork, help omelette start rolling away from handle to opposite side of the pan. Use fork delicately, never pressing, to preserve fluffiness.

6. Raise pan to almost vertical to complete rolling of the omelette out of the pan onto a warm plate. It should only be 95 percent cooked, as the inside continues to cook for a short while on its own after you take it off the heat.

Steps 3 through 6 should take only one minute, and should produce one perfect omelette, golden in color, light in texture, and voluptuous as a sex goddess. If at first you don't succeed, hurry over to Serendipity and have a caviar and sour cream omelette. And try again. As Beard himself would have said, "Break an egg."

Fines Herbes Omelette

Prepare as for a basic omelette, adding 1 teaspoon mixed dried herbs to the eggs and whisking before cooking.

Cheddar Omelette

Prepare a plain omelette. When it is ready to be rolled, sprinkle a generous handful of grated sharp cheddar cheese over the omelette. Cook for an extra second or two to melt the cheese, roll, and serve, garnished with parsley.

Caviar and Sour Cream Omelette

Over a plain omelette, heap 2 tablespoons of sour cream. On top of this, heap a generous tablespoon of red or black caviar and garnish with parsley.

Curried Mushroom Omelette

Approximately ½ cup chicken stock
1 cup sliced mushrooms (¼-inch slices)
1 teaspoon good curry powder

1 to 2 tablespoons butter
1 small onion, sliced on the slant
Parsley

1. In a medium saucepan, cook stock, mushrooms, and curry powder for 5 minutes.
2. Meanwhile, in a small skillet, place butter and onion and sauté until golden brown. Then add the onion and butter to the mushroom mixture.
3. Let it cook to a light boil, then mix and remove from heat.

4. Spoon ½ cup curried mushrooms and its sauce diagonally across a plain omelette and garnish with parsley.

Chutney and Sour Cream Omelette

Over a plain omelette, heap 2 tablespoons of sour cream. Over this, heap a generous tablespoon of Sun Brand chutney.

Cream Cheese and Rhubarb-Ginger Jam Omelette

Have ready a block of cream cheese approximately ¾-inch thick by 6 inches long and slightly flattened. Cheese should be softened at room temperature. Lay cream cheese on the omelette before it is rolled, leaving the omelette in the pan for a few seconds to melt the cheese. Spread 2 tablespoons of Baxter's Rhubarb-and-Ginger Jam diagonally over the top of the omelette.

Chili Omelette

Across a plain omelette, pour one small ladleful of chili (page 83). Serve with a side helping of sour cream and chopped purple onions.

Ham and Cheese Omelette

Place 6 or 8 nice-sized chunks of baked ham in an omelette, before it is rolled. Then proceed as in cheddar omelette.

White Asparagus and Jarlsberg Cheese Omelette

Proceed as in ham and cheese omelette, substituting 3 or 4 stalks of white asparagus (in season) and grated Jarlsberg for the ham and cheese.

Sausage and Peppers Omelette

Proceed as above, using 2 sausages and ½ pepper, sliced (which have both been sautéed in butter first), in omelette before folding.

Hangover Omelette

For one omelette, coarsely chop one green chili from a can of Ashley's green chili peppers and scatter it diagonally across one plain omelette before it is rolled. That way, each bite will contain the bite of chili pepper. Sprinkle a generous quantity of grated cheddar cheese over the omelette and let it cook a couple of seconds more. When the cheese melts, roll the omelette, first one side, then the other and turn onto a warm plate. Spread 2 tablespoons of sour cream diagonally across the top and garnish with parsley.

Salad Days

(*continued from page 54*)

the buff. A stick of dynamite couldn't have gotten them to their feet faster. They beat a hasty retreat, leaving Big Bird with a hefty tip.

When it comes to difficult cases, Stephen Bruce is Mr. Savoir Faire. A pair of overdressed Yuppies made an entrance one night, flourishing the status-seekers' wine, a bottle of Mouton Rothschild.

Serendipity is two feet too close to a church for a liquor license, so it's always been the "in" thing to bring your own. These two were so imperious in demanding that their wine be uncorked and served that the waiter, who was accustomed only to *vin ordinaire*, became unnerved, and shoved the cork in instead of out.

Specks of crumbled cork floated in the wine. There were red faces and cries of outrage. Stephen coolly assessed the situation, picked up the bottle, and disappeared into the kitchen. A strainer and a decanter and voilà! Baron de Rothschild himself couldn't have done better. He poured it with such aplomb that they were pacified. "I see that you strained our hundred-and-fifty-dollar wine," said one of them approvingly. Stephen had had quite enough of these parvenus. "Yes, I did," he shot back, "through my jockey shorts."

Stephen Bruce's dash and mustache were much envied and hopefully emulated by Richard W., a fawning Jack-of-all-trades who all but salaamed at his Lordships' bidding, and whom the waiters teasingly referred to as "Stephen's brother." When Stephen sported a Salvador Dali "antenna" mustache, its ends extravagantly waxed and curled and pointing heavenward, Stephen's brother affected one, too. When Stephen became fixated on the close-cropped cut of the Hercule Poirot mustache, and clipped his handlebars, his brother was slightly discomfited, but soon followed his example.

For thirty years, a self-effacing wisp of a costume designer shared a dusty third-floor broom closet on one of Serendipity's upper floors, with three filing cabinets full of vitamin pills. A card-carrying hypochondriac, she popped pills from A to Z while slaving devotedly at her masters' service, without so much as a whit of public recognition. She finally succumbed to one of the diseases she tried so desperately to avoid. Even as she breathed her last, her shoulder was to the wheel, hand-addressing the thousands of Christmas cards on Serendipity's list.

Pincus Cashman, a character right out of the Keystone Cops, was Serendipity's attorney. Never mind that their landlady loved "her boys," and practically gave them their building. Mr. Cashman made out the papers, and that made him omnipotent in their eyes. Their legal counsel in all things, he managed to queer Serendipity in dealings with the William Morris Agency, who dubbed him a well-meaning shyster. He placed a copyright on the name Serendipity for restaurant and boutique use. In spite of his precautions, Serendipities proliferate. There is a Serendipity Modeling Agency, a Serendipity Record Company. Matches and menus are evidence of a Serendipity Restaurant in London. There are Serendipity boutiques in Rome and Mykonos, and Serendipity clones around the world. The strange-sounding name is now an international buzz word.

For a spell, Molinero's parrot was content with the coffeehouse menu, cappuccino or espresso served with Aunt Buba's sand tarts or Miss Milton's lovely things. An incurable "flaneur," she stayed till all hours, which gave her an appetite for more substantial fare. Once again, Polly began to squawk, (*continued on page 91*)

Chicken Julia

The salad that put Serendipity on New York's lunch map made its debut as an entrée on a table d'hôte menu in the early sixties. It came with juice or soup, a small salad, dessert, and a beverage, all for $3.75. Times have changed, but "time cannot wither nor custom stale" Chicken Julia's infinite appeal.

1 teaspoon dry mustard
1/2 cup sugar
1 teaspoon salt
2 tablespoons flour
1/4 cup cold water
1 1/4 cups boiling water
2 eggs
1/2 cup vinegar
4 tablespoons butter

1 3/4 cups sour cream
4 cups cooked chicken cut into 1/2-inch
*   cubes*
2 cups finely minced celery
Bed of lettuce
Garnish of sliced avocado, tomato
*   wedges, sprigs of watercress, toasted*
*   almonds*

1. In a bowl, dissolve the mustard, sugar, salt, and flour in cold water, and add the boiling water.

2. In the top of a double boiler, beat the eggs and vinegar. Add the first mixture. Cook and stir over boiling water until thick and smooth.

3. Add the butter; mix and cool. Pour into an electric mixer bowl and add the sour cream. Mix thoroughly at low speed. Chill.

4. Dress the 4 cups of cooked chicken cubes and 2 cups of minced celery in this dressing. Serve one cut of this chicken salad per portion on a bed of lettuce, garnished with thin slices of avocado, small tomato wedges, a sprig of watercress, and a generous sprinkling of toasted almonds.

Serves 6 to 8.

Shrimp Salad

(See Shrimp Salad Sandwich, page 57.)

1. Salad is served on a bed of lettuce, one cup of shrimp salad topped with one whole shrimp, surrounded with cucumber slices.

Serves 1.

Shrimp Stuffed Avocado

1. Cut a ripe avocado in half, remove pit, and stuff both halves with Shrimp Salad (page 57). Top with one whole shrimp and garnish with cucumber slices.

Serves 1.

Vanessa's Revenge: Turkey with Artichoke Hearts

1. Follow the recipe for Chicken Julia, page 71, substituting cooked turkey for chicken.

2. Serve a cupful (8 ounces) of turkey salad on a bed of lettuce, garnished with tomato wedges and artichoke hearts.

Serves 1.

Pasta Fortuna Salad

12 ounces fresh pasta
2 7-ounce cans tuna
½ bunch fresh basil
2 green peppers, diced
2 fresh tomatoes, diced

½ purple onion, diced
1 clove garlic, ½ chopped finely, ½
  reserved for rubbing bowl
1 cup Vinaigrette Dressing

1. Cook pasta al dente, rinse after cooking, and set aside.
2. Drain 2 cans of tuna and break up any large chunks.
3. Mix all ingredients (including ½ clove chopped garlic) together and keep chilled until ready to serve. At serving time, rub a wooden serving bowl with the second half clove of garlic, and toss the salad with enough of the Vinaigrette Dressing (page 78) to moisten.

Serves 6 at lunch.

Avocado and Grapefruit Salad

1 ripe avocado
1 perfect grapefruit

Cored apple wedges
Hulled fresh strawberries

1. Peel avocado and slice into 8 wedges.
2. Peel grapefruit and remove membranes.
3. For one serving, arrange 4 alternate slices of avocado and grapefruit. Garnish with cored Granny Smith apple wedges and fresh strawberries. Dress with Lemon-Lime or Curry-Chutney dressing (page 76).

Serves 2.

Spinach Salad

1 pound bacon, chopped
1 clove garlic
1 pound fresh spinach, tough stems
   removed, washed and drained

1 pound fresh mushrooms, thinly sliced

1. Cook the bacon in a skillet, not too well done, and drain on absorbent paper.
2. Rub wooden salad bowl with garlic. Toss the clean, dry spinach leaves, mushrooms, and chopped (or crumbled) bacon bits with the following dressing.

Spinach Salad Dressing

4 tablespoons red wine vinegar
3 pinches tarragon
3 pinches basil
3 pinches savory
1 clove fresh garlic, pressed
1 tablespoon honey

1 teaspoon granulated sugar
½ teaspoon salt
½ teaspoon freshly ground pepper
½ cup olive oil
1 tablespoon freshly grated Parmesan
   cheese

1. Combine all ingredients except the oil and cheese in a blender and mix at slow speed.
2. Slowly dribble in olive oil until mixture thickens; season to taste.
3. When all the oil is added, add the cheese, whisk well with a wire whisk. Dress the salad, toss, and serve.

Serves 4 to 6.

Boiled Beef Salad

Boil a 1-pound cut of chuck until tender. Chill and dice it into ½-inch cubes. Prepare the following dressing in the proportions given, and use as much of it as you will need to anoint the beef. Cover and store the rest.

1 cup mayonnaise
1 cup sour cream
1/3 cup horseradish
1/3 cup wine vinegar
1/3 cup capers

1 smallish purple onion, cut in thin
   rings
Salt and freshly ground black pepper,
   to taste

1. Whisk ingredients together well with a wire whisk and dribble over beef salad. Your eye will tell you when to stop. Toss well and serve.

Serves 4.

Bean Sprout and Mushroom Salad

4 cups drained bean sprouts
2 cups thinly sliced mushrooms
1/4 cup wine vinegar
1/2 cup applesauce
1/4 teaspoon freshly ground black
   pepper

1/2 cup sugar
1/4 cup soy sauce
1/2 cup vegetable oil

1. Toss the bean sprouts and mushrooms in a salad bowl.
2. Blend all dressing ingredients together well and pour over the bean sprouts and mushrooms. This combines sweet and tart and is quite unusual.

Serves 6.

A Serendip Salad

Combine 3 of your favorite greens, like Bibb, endive, and romaine, torn into bite-size pieces and tossed together with a generous amount of coriander seeds. Pile into a salad bowl with fresh pineapple chunks, sliced dates, and thinly sliced purple onion rings. Serve with the following dressings:

Serves 1 to 100, depending on quantity of greens.

Lemon-Lime Dressing

⅓ cup lemon juice, freshly squeezed
1½ tablespoons fresh lime juice
⅔ cup salad oil

1 teaspoon salt
1 teaspoon paprika
1 tablespoon honey

1. Blend ingredients and refrigerate in a covered jar. Shake well before using.

Makes a fraction over 1 cup.

Curry-Chutney Dressing

¾ cup salad oil
¼ cup vinegar
1 teaspoon salt
1 teaspoon sugar
½ teaspoon paprika

¼ teaspoon dry mustard
Dash of freshly ground pepper
2 tablespoons chopped chutney
2 hard-cooked eggs, finely chopped
½ teaspoon curry powder

1. Blend ingredients thoroughly and refrigerate in a covered jar. Shake well before using.

Makes 1½ cups.

Hot Potato Salad

6 medium-sized waxy potatoes
4 strips minced bacon
¼ cup chopped onions
¼ cup chopped celery
1 chopped dill pickle
¼ cup water or stock

½ cup vinegar
½ teaspoon sugar
½ teaspoon salt
⅛ teaspoon paprika
¼ teaspoon dry mustard
Chopped fresh parsley or chives

1. In a covered saucepan, cook potatoes in their jackets until tender. Peel and slice while they are hot.

2. In a skillet, sauté the bacon until brown, add and sauté the onion, celery, and pickle.

3. In another pot, heat to the boiling point the water or stock, vinegar, sugar, salt, paprika, and dry mustard.

4. Pour these ingredients into the skillet. Combine them with the potatoes and serve at once with chopped fresh parsley or chopped fresh chives.

Serves 6.

Aunt Tutti's Fruited Chicken Salad

While still in knee pants, Calvin hitchhiked from Hazen to Evening Shade, Arkansas, and headed straight for his auntie's kitchen. This dish is guaranteed to make a growing boy go to any lengths to get more.

3 tablespoons chutney, finely chopped
¼ teaspoon ground cardamom
2 tablespoons fresh lime juice
⅓ cup mayonnaise
⅓ cup plain yogurt
Salt and pepper, to taste
3 cups cold cooked chicken, cut into ½-inch cubes (about 2 whole chicken breasts)

1 mango, peeled and cut into ½-inch chunks
½ honeydew melon, seeded and scooped into balls
2 green onions, minced
1 bunch watercress
Kiwi and raspberries

1. In a large bowl, combine chutney, cardamom, lime juice, mayonnaise, yogurt, salt, and pepper. Add chicken, mango, melon, and onions. Toss the salad well. Place in plastic container.

2. Wash and dry the watercress and cut away the tough stems. Serve the salad on a bed of cress. Garnish with slices of kiwi and raspberries.

Serves 6.

Haricot Vert and Tomato Salad

1½ pounds of fresh haricots verts,
   ends trimmed
1 red onion, peeled and thinly sliced
3 ripe tomatoes, sliced

½ cup Lemon-Lime, Curry-Chutney
   Dressing (page 76), or Vinaigrette
2 tablespoons chopped parsley

Bring a large saucepan of salted water to a boil. Add the haricots verts and cook 3 to 5 minutes, then drain. Plunge into ice water to stop the cooking process. When cool, drain well. Place in a plastic bowl with the onions and tomatoes and chill. At mealtime, combine the dressing and parsley and drizzle over the salad. Toss gently and transfer it to a serving bowl. (In the absence of the more delicate haricots verts, by all means use string beans.)

Serves 6.

Vinaigrette Dressing

1 tablespoon prepared Dijon mustard
4 tablespoons red wine vinegar
1 teaspoon granulated sugar
½ teaspoon salt

½ teaspoon freshly ground black
   pepper
1 teaspoon minced Italian parsley
1 teaspoon chopped fresh basil
½ cup olive oil

1. Measure mustard into a bowl. Whisk in vinegar, sugar, salt, pepper, and herbs to taste.
2. Continue to whisk mixture while slowly dribbling in olive oil until the mixture thickens. Season to taste. Cover until ready to use. Though it is best just after it is made, whisking again just before serving will freshen it up.

Makes about ¾ cup.

A Carousel of Casseroles

Curried Chicken Almondine

One pound package of thin noodles
A fresh, young 2½–3 pound stewing
  chicken

3 stalks of celery with leaves
2 small yellow onions, quartered

1. Cook the noodles in advance in salted water, and set aside.

2. Place chicken, leafy celery, and onions in a pot with enough salted water to cover them, bring to a boil, and simmer until chicken is tender.

3. Strain stock and set aside. Separate chicken from bone in good-sized pieces.

Curry Sauce for Curried Chicken Almondine

2 tablespoons butter
2 small onions, finely sliced
¼ pound sliced mushrooms
Small bunch of parsley
1 cup heavy cream
1 cup chicken stock

2 tablespoons flour
2 heaping teaspoons (or more to taste)
  curry powder
Salt and freshly ground pepper
Dash of sherry
Handful of sliced, toasted almonds

1. Melt butter in a skillet and sauté onions till golden, then add mushrooms and parsley. Combine well, then transfer to a saucepan and add the cream, stock, flour, curry powder, and seasoning to taste.

2. Simmer over a low heat, stirring until the sauce is the consistency of heavy soup.

3. Line an ovenproof casserole with noodles. Cover them with deboned, skinless chicken chunks. Top the whole ensemble with the curry sauce. Add 2 tablespoons of chicken stock and a dash of sherry. Sprinkle generously with toasted almonds and bake at 350 degrees for 10 or 12 minutes.

Weight watchers, please turn the page while 6 of us indulge.

Burgundy Beef

2 tablespoons butter

2 pounds lean stewing beef cut into
1½-inch cubes

1 tablespoon flour

Salt, pepper

½ pound small onions, sliced not too
fine

2 carrots

2 shallots

1 clove garlic, minced not too fine

1 teaspoon thyme

1 teaspoon marjoram

1 bay leaf

½ cup Madeira

1½ cups burgundy wine

Liquor glass of brandy

1. Melt and heat butter in a heavy pan and brown beef on all sides. (Do not overcrowd pan.) Remove meat as it is browned.

2. Add flour, stir until brown. Add salt and pepper. Then stir in onions, carrots, shallots, garlic, thyme, marjoram, bay leaf. Combine well and transfer with the meat to an ovenproof casserole.

3. Add Madeira and burgundy and enough water to bring the liquid level with the meat. Cover and simmer 3 or 4 hours until the meat is tender.

4. One-half hour before serving, add the brandy. Drain out the vegetables, press them through a sieve, and add the puree to the gravy, to thicken it. Serve on a bed of wild rice.

Serves 6.

Shepherd's Pie

The Pastry Shell:

1 cup flour

¼ teaspoon salt

4 tablespoons butter

2 tablespoons vegetable shortening

3 tablespoons cold water

1 egg yolk, beaten with 1 tablespoon
water

1. Mix flour with salt and work in butter and shortening.

2. Slowly sprinkle cold water over the pastry and mix with a fork. Gather dough into a ball and refrigerate for 30 minutes.

The Pie Filling:

3 pounds of lean beef, ground	1/2 cup Madeira
2 carrots, peeled and sliced	1/2 teaspoon hot sauce
1 3/4 green peppers, in 9 slices	1/4 teaspoon ground black pepper
2 tomatoes in 6 slices each	1 teaspoon paprika
1 onion, diced	1/2 teaspoon garlic powder
6 mushrooms, chopped	1/2 teaspoon cumin
1 small can pimentos, diced	1/2 teaspoon sugar
1/2 small #1 can chili peppers, diced	1 1/2 teaspoons oregano
1/4 cup raisins	1 1/2 teaspoons allspice
1/4 cup soy sauce	1/2 teaspoon ground cloves
Juice of 1 lemon	1 teaspoon salt or to taste
3 tablespoons brandy	1/2 package frozen petits pois

3. Roll out the dough for a 9-inch pie pan. Fit into the pan and brush with egg yolk–water mixture. Refrigerate while preparing Shepherd's Pie Filling.

4. Heat beef in heavy skillet and cook until almost half brown.

5. Add the carrots, peppers, tomatoes, onion, and mushrooms and cook all together until beef is brown.

6. Add pimentos, green chili peppers, raisins, and soy sauce to mixture, stir and continue cooking.

7. When mixture starts to boil, add lemon juice, brandy, Madeira, hot sauce, and spices. Let mixture boil for 10 minutes, stirring often.

8. Remove from heat, add thawed peas and mix well. Strain to remove most of the liquid.

9. Fill the pastry shell with what remains after the liquid has been removed. Top with the Serendipitous Mashed Potatoes (page 109), and sprinkle with a handful of shredded cheddar cheese. Bake in a 375-degree oven for 30 minutes.

Serves 6 generously.

Chili for Thirty-five of Your Dearest Friends

10 pounds of beef chuck, ground
3 tablespoons minced fresh garlic
4 onions, diced
3/4 tablespoon salt
1 tablespoon freshly ground black pepper
3 tablespoons ground cumin
4 tablespoons chili powder
4 tablespoons basil

4 tablespoons dried oregano
1 teaspoon sugar
3 cans, 16 ounces each, dark red kidney beans, drained
6 pounds pureed tomatoes, about 5 cans, each 2 pounds, 3 ounces
Sour cream, chopped purple onion, grated cheddar cheese for garnish

1. In a very large soup kettle, brown the beef with the minced garlic.
2. After the beef is cooked, strain to remove fat.
3. In a skillet, heat beef fat and cook onions in the fat until they are soft.
4. Add onions to the beef, along with the spices and sugar. Mix well to combine.
5. Add the kidney beans and the puree. Stir well and simmer, uncovered, for 15 minutes.
6. Taste and correct seasonings. Serve with separate bowls of sour cream, chopped purple onion, and grated cheddar cheese and let your friends garnish as they please. Serve with blue corn chips,* Blue Spoon Bread (page 120), and salad.

Zen Hash

1/4 pound butter
2 small onions
1 cup vegetable oil
7 zucchini, washed, trimmed, quartered lengthwise, and cut into 2-inch strips
1 cup plus 1 tablespoon soy sauce
Peel of 3/4 of a lemon

1/4 teaspoon hot sauce
1/2 teaspoon black pepper
1/2 teaspoon garlic powder
1 carrot, grated
1 handful grated cheese
1/2 pound spinach, stems removed, cleaned, washed, dried

1. Melt butter; add onions and cook until soft. Add oil.

* Blue Heaven Corn Chips are available at Grace's Marketplace, 1237 Third Avenue, New York, NY.

2. To this mixture, add the zucchini, soy sauce, lemon peel, hot sauce, and spices. Stir well, combining all flavors.

3. Remove from the heat, add carrots, cheese, and spinach. Mix together until all the ingredients are well blended.

4. Serve over brown rice, in a casserole.

Serves 6.

Lobster Casserole

3 tablespoons butter
3 tablespoons flour
1½ cups milk
½ cup grated Tillamook cheese
3 tablespoons sherry
Salt and pepper

¾ cup whole walnuts
1½ cups lobster meat, cut into bite-
   sized chunks
4 hard-boiled eggs, sliced
½ pound sautéed mushrooms
Breadcrumbs

1. Mix butter and flour over a low fire and then add milk, stirring until thick. Add grated cheese, sherry, salt, and pepper. Simmer awhile. Set aside.

2. Butter baking dish. Place alternate layers of lobster, eggs, and mushrooms with walnuts sprinkled throughout. Cover with sauce and top with a thin coating of breadcrumbs. Place in oven at 350 degrees for about an hour. It's even better than it sounds.

Serves 6.

Beans and Rice Pretty Baby

"I love you once,
I love you twice;
I love you more
than beans and rice,"
sang Brooke Shields in Louis Malle's masterpiece, *Pretty Baby*. To Brooke, the prettiest baby who ever graced the tables of Serendipity, we offer proof that though the red lights no longer blaze on Basin Street, the fragrance of beans and rice lingers on at Serendipity 3.

1½ pounds red kidney beans
1 tablespoon olive oil
1 large onion, chopped
1 ham steak, about 1 pound, cut into
  ½-inch cubes
3 cloves garlic
1½ teaspoons dried thyme
1½ teaspoons dried oregano
1 bay leaf
½ pound bacon cut into small pieces
1 ham bone

¼ cup tomato juice
Salt and freshly ground pepper, to
  taste
1 teaspoon Tabasco sauce
1 pound pepperoni or Danish salami,
  cut into ½-inch cubes
2 cups raw rice, cooked separately and
  steamed dry
1 Spanish or red onion
Olive oil
Red wine vinegar

1. Wash beans, discarding broken ones.

2. Heat olive oil in a large pot and sauté the chopped onion until it is soft, but not brown. Add the beans and all the rest of the ingredients except the pepperoni, rice, and Spanish onion.

3. Add enough water to cover the beans. Bring to a boil, cover tightly, and lower heat to simmer. Stir frequently (every 10 minutes or so), and add a little more water as needed. Usually, beans take 1½ to 2 hours to become soft, yet remain whole. As beans cook, watch for the sauce to become quite thick.

4. About 12 minutes before the beans are fully cooked, add the pepperoni.

5. Meanwhile, cook the rice separately, making sure it is dry, but not mushy.

6. Chop the Spanish onion into small pieces.

7. Serve the beans on a bed of rice and offer onions separately, as a garnish. Oil and vinegar are traditionally offered, separately, to be added as desired. A nice variation would be one of the two Serendipity salad dressings, Lemon-Lime or Curry-Chutney (page 76).

Serves 8.

Deviled Crabmeat

1 pound crabmeat
1½ cups rolled cracker crumbs
¾ cup finely diced celery
¾ cup chopped onion
½ cup melted butter
¼ cup milk

1 teaspoon dry mustard
½ teaspoon salt
Few grains of cayenne pepper
2 tablespoons chopped parsley
1 tablespoon chopped green pepper

1. Combine the crabmeat with the crumbs, celery, and onion in a large bowl and moisten with melted butter and milk.

2. Season with mustard, salt, cayenne, parsley, and green pepper, and mix thoroughly.

3. Transfer contents to a buttered, ovenproof casserole and bake in a 350-degree oven for about half an hour.

Serves 4 to 6.

Hot Tamale Pie

Although most early Serendipity dishes were Southern in origin, this James Beard creation went south all the way, to Mexico, for its roots.

The Filling:

1 large onion, minced
1 large green pepper, minced
1 or 2 crushed garlic cloves
3 tablespoons margarine or butter
1½ pounds ground beef
1 teaspoon salt

1 to 4 teaspoons ground black pepper
 (or to taste)
1 tablespoon chili powder
1 #2 can tomatoes
1 cup chopped and pitted ripe olives

The Pie Shell:

4 cups boiling water
1 teaspoon salt

2 cups white cornmeal
1 handful grated cheddar cheese

1. Sauté onion, pepper, and garlic in margarine or butter in a heavy skillet.

2. Add ground beef, salt, pepper, and chili powder and cook over low heat for 20 to 30 minutes. Stir frequently to prevent burning.

3. Add the can of tomatoes, which have been finely mashed. Bring stove up to a high heat for a few minutes.

4. Reduce heat and simmer over a very low flame for 10 minutes. When the cornmeal mush crust (below) is ready, add olives to this mixture just before transferring it to the pie shell.

5. Mix the boiling water with the salt and let it come to a rolling boil.

6. Meanwhile, mix the white cornmeal thoroughly with 2 cups of cold water (this is the secret of good results with the mush), and add to the boiling water.

7. Cook in a heavy pan over low heat until thick, stirring to prevent sticking.

8. Spread the mush over the bottom and sides of a well-greased baking dish (about 10 by 15 inches). Next, add the meat mixture. Top the meat with a thin layer of cornmeal mush.

9. Sprinkle the pie with grated cheddar cheese and bake in a moderate oven (350 degrees) for 30 minutes.

Serves 8 to 10.

Pinto Beans with Chili and Sausage

1 pound pink pinto beans
1 bay leaf
1 onion stuck with 2 cloves
Salt, to taste
¼ pound bacon, cut thick
4 cloves garlic, finely chopped
1 cup shallots, finely chopped

1 teaspoon thyme
1 teaspoon ground cumin
4 tablespoons chili powder
1 cup tomato paste
2 tablespoons wine vinegar
2 pounds pork sausages, preferably
  chorizos

1. Soak the beans overnight. Drain, and add fresh water to reach 1½ inches above the beans. Add the bay leaf, onion, and salt to taste. Bring to a boil in a large pot and cook until the beans are just tender. Drain, and reserve the liquid.

2. Meanwhile, sauté the bacon, which has been cut into small cubes. Remove the bacon, and add garlic and shallots to the fat. Cook till just soft.

3. Add thyme, cumin, chili powder, tomato paste, and vinegar, and blend with the beans, adding about 1 cup of the bean liquid.

4. Transfer the entire mixture to an ovenproof casserole, and cover with its own cover or a piece of foil. Bake at 350 degrees for 1 hour.

5. Meanwhile, poach the sausages in water for 10 minutes, and add them to the casserole. Return the casserole to the oven until the sausages are browned, about 35 to 40 minutes longer. Add more bean liquid during the baking process if the casserole seems dry.

Serves 6 to 8.

Corned Beef Hash

1 pound cooked corned beef
3 boiled potatoes, chopped coarsely
1 small onion, chopped coarsely
1/2 teaspoon salt
1/2 teaspoon pepper

Pinch of ginger
Pinch of allspice
6 tablespoons beef fat, cream, or water
Butter

1. Chop the cooked corned beef coarsely. Combine with the potatoes and onion in a large bowl and mix well. Season with salt, freshly ground pepper, ginger, and allspice and mix thoroughly.

2. Heat the beef fat in a heavy cast-iron skillet. Transfer the contents of the bowl to the skillet, pressing them down firmly with a spatula or pancake turner. Cook slowly, over a low heat, mixing well with a fork for the first few minutes.

3. Press down with a spatula again, and continue cooking over low heat. Add a little boiling water or hot cream and let this cook dry. There should be a nice crust forming on the bottom of the hash.

4. Dot the top with butter and run it under the broiler for a few minutes to brown a bit. Using a spatula, fold the hash over and roll it out on a hot platter, crusty side up. Serve with poached or fried eggs. The traditional accompaniments are coleslaw and chili sauce.

Serves 6.

Crab Quiche Bettina

1 cup leeks, cut into 1-inch slices
1 cup sliced mushrooms
1 tablespoon butter
6 to 8 ounces crabmeat, flaked, bones
  removed

1½ cups heavy cream
4 eggs
½ teaspoon salt
Dash of freshly ground black pepper
1 tablespoon finely chopped parsley

1. Cook leeks in boiling salted water for 10 minutes. Drain.

2. Sauté mushrooms in butter in a skillet for 4 to 5 minutes. Add the leeks to the mushrooms and mix well.

3. Have prepared Pastry Shell ready (see recipe for Shepherd's Pie, page 81). Sprinkle mushrooms and leeks on the bottom of the pastry shell. Top with crabmeat. Mix cream, eggs, salt, and pepper together and pour mixture over the crabmeat. Sprinkle chopped parsley over all.

4. Bake quiche in a 375-degree oven for 30 minutes approximately.

Serves 6.

(*continued from page 71*)
"Polly wanna pizza. Polly wanna pasta."

Serendipity 3 put Polly's order on the back burner and hastened to James Beard, cooking guru extraordinaire, for omelette lessons. "It's all in the wrist," he told them. "Never mind how many eggs you break. Practice, practice, practice." It soon became clear that as an omeleteer, Stephen was a born fashion designer. So Patch and Calvin busied themselves with the pan until it soon became clear they needed a cook. Hattie McDaniels was otherwise occupied, so they found the next best.

Miss Julia was a treasure of the most serendipitous sort. Not only could she turn out the delicious "Depression recipes" from Aunt Buba's and Miss Milton's boardinghouse kitchen in Little Rock, she introduced Southern specialties of her own. Humming gospel songs, she brought forth her greatest triumph, Chicken Julia. Her greatest flop was burning a pecan pie while she primped in her new Easter bonnet. Stephen did one for her every year, each spectacular enough to start a flame in anyone's pecan pie.

At the start, she and Patch danced the two-step when they had fifteen in for lunch. It took a *New York Times* food critique to bring the crowds, and with them, celebrities like Lena Horne. Miss Julia kept an eye out for browsers in the General Store, calling, "Front!" to keep her gentlemen on the qui vive. Cooking all day and dancing all night took its toll. She decided to settle down and get married. As a legacy, she left the perfect job to her younger sister.

Miss Essie Vaughn created a chocolate drink called Awful Awful, but her claim to fame was Lemon Icebox Pie. A key ingredient was Carnation Milk. The main attraction of Carnation was its premium, offering a kolinsky fur piece in exchange for a thousand Carnation labels. She piled on the whipped cream, making sure that lemon pie was numero uno in demand. A thousand and one lemon pies later, at her retirement party, Miss Essie arrived, swathed in kolinsky. Never minding the August heat wave, she was in kolinsky heaven.

Julio Hernandez, a roly-poly emigré from Honduras, blessed Calvin before he went off to make his TV appearances. Julio played priest, chef, and comedian, in turn, particularly when Stephen ventured into his domain. Unbeknownst to Stephen, this jolly fat man would follow him out of the kitchen, doing an exaggerated impersonation of his elegantly graceful walk, while the waiters smothered their chuckles. Julio listened to impure talk. He thought impure thoughts. He felt remorse. "I'm off to a monastery," he said.

"Don't try to find me." He is mourned to this day. He instilled the fear of God. When Calvin goes on TV, he lights a candle at Saint Patrick's first. Just in case. After enjoying a hearty repast, Polly began to squawk again (*continued on page 97*), (*continued on page 97*)

Vegetable Pizza

2 tablespoons butter
2 or 3 tablespoons olive oil
3/4 cup sliced mushrooms
1/3 cup minced onions
1/4 cup minced green pepper
1/4 cup minced celery
1 teaspoon garlic powder
1/4 bay leaf, crumbled
Pinch of thyme
1/4 teaspoon salt

1/4 teaspoon freshly ground black
  pepper
1/4 cup burgundy wine
1/2 cup tomato paste
32-ounce can whole tomatoes
4 7-inch whole wheat pizza crusts (see
  page 93)
1 pound Munster cheese, cut in 8 2-
  ounce slices
1 pound Jarlsberg cheese, grated

1. Combine butter and oil in a large pot over medium heat.

2. When the butter is melted, add the vegetables, stirring constantly, and sautéeing until the onion is transparent and all the vegetables are limp.

3. Add all the spices and mix well.

4. Add the burgundy and the tomato paste, stirring to be sure of a thorough blend of flavors.

5. With the tomatoes still in the can, mash them with a wire whisk until they are broken into small pieces.

6. Add the broken tomatoes and mix well. Turn the heat down to low and simmer for 30 minutes, stirring occasionally.

7. Heat the sauce on 4 whole wheat pizza crusts in Serendipity-sized portions. Cover each with 2 slices of Munster cheese and sprinkle with a generous handful of Jarlsberg. Bake the pizza on the bottom shelf of a preheated 500-degree electric oven or on the floor of a 500-degree gas oven for 10 or 15 minutes, or until the crust is golden brown.

Serves 4.

Whole Wheat Pizza Crusts

1¼-ounce package (2½ teaspoons)
  active dry yeast
½ teaspoon sugar
½ teaspoon salt
1¼ cups hot water

1 cup pastry flour
1 cup whole wheat flour
1 cup all-purpose flour
2 tablespoons olive oil

1. Mix the yeast, sugar, and ¼ cup of hot water in a large bowl, and let it stand until the mixture foams (about 10 minutes).

2. In a second bowl, combine salt and 1 cup of hot water and set aside.

3. Measure and combine the 3 flours thoroughly. When the yeast proofs and becomes foamy, stir in the flour mixture, the salted hot water (1 cup), and the olive oil, continuing to stir. Blend the mixture until it forms a dough. If dough is sticky to the touch, add a small amount of wheat flour and continue mixing.

4. Place the dough in a large mixing bowl and seal tightly with plastic wrap. Set in a warm place, *not on a hot oven*! until the dough has risen (approximately 1 hour), and is double in bulk.

5. Remove plastic wrap and punch dough so it falls back down. Sprinkle 4 7-inch pizza tins lightly with vegetable shortening. Divide dough into 4 round balls.

6. Sprinkle wheat flour on a dry slab or surface, and rub some on the rolling pin. Roll each dough ball ¼ inch larger than the tin and fill tins, crimping the edges.

Serves 4.

Sausage Pizza

This Serendipity favorite is a duplicate of Vegetable Pizza (page 92), with the addition of 8 to 10 slices of the sausage of your choice, dotted atop the cheese before baking.

If you are in the middle of making pizza, and are too hungry to complete the operation, here's where you can stop: At the end of step 6 in the Vegetable Pizza recipe, cover the sauce tightly with plastic wrap and refrigerate; at the completion of step 6 in the pizza crust recipe, you can do the same, thanks to plastic wrap and the refrigerator.

Now you can come into Serendipity for a pizza break, and take up where you left off tomorrow.

Pasta Magnani

The heroine of *The Rose Tattoo* suffered from an olive-oil-country malady, child-bearing hips. But her passion for Pasta Puttanesca remained unabated. So she arrived at a compromise, one that didn't affect the racy lady-of-the-evening flavor of the pasta, but did cut down a bit on the calories. Warning: One cup of this pasta is all you're allowed if you're seriously hip-watching.

1 large Bermuda onion
4 to 5 stalks celery
2 to 3 cloves garlic
1 small can of anchovy fillets, coarsely chopped, including the oil
1/4 cup water
1/4 cup white or red wine
1 28-ounce can Italian tomatoes, packed in puree

3 tablespoons capers
1 teaspoon fresh basil, chopped, or more according to taste
1/4 cup chopped Italian parsley, and more for garnish
A generous grinding of black pepper
6 spicy Italian or Greek olives
1 pound green angel hair pasta

1. Chop the onion, celery, and garlic very fine with a food processor or blender. If they get "mushy," that's all to the good. Sauté them with the anchovy fillets in water and wine over a high heat, until the liquid boils down and the consistency is thick.

2. Add tomatoes, capers, basil, parsley, and black pepper and reduce heat; simmer for 20 minutes. Add the olives while the sauce is simmering, and stir frequently to make sure all the flavors are evenly dispersed.

3. Meanwhile, bring 4 quarts of water to a rolling boil in a large pot. Add salt. At the very last minute, stir in the angel hair pasta, which takes only 60 seconds to cook. Test a strand to make sure it is tender, but "al dente"; drain immediately and transfer to 4 heated plates. Ladle the sauce over the hot pasta and serve with freshly grated Parmesan cheese. Use a little restraint, and limit yourself to one tablespoonful of cheese, please.

Serves 6.

Pesto with Prosciutto

Summertime, when the living is easy and the basil is plentiful, that's when pesto is as stylish as a tan. Try it on a mound of multicolored (tomato-spinach-and-wheat) pasta,* crunchy with pine nuts, flecked with shavings of pink prosciutto.

2 cups fresh basil leaves, washed and patted dry
3 or 4 garlic cloves, minced extra fine
½ cup shelled walnuts
1 cup olive oil

1 cup freshly grated Parmesan cheese
Salt and black pepper, freshly ground
½ cup pine nuts
½ cup finely shredded prosciutto ham

1. In a food processor or a blender, chop the basil well, then add the garlic and walnuts and continue chopping.
2. Continue blending while adding the olive oil in a slow, steady stream.
3. Add the cheese, salt, and pepper, and blend. Shut off the motor and fold in the whole pine nuts and prosciutto. Transfer to a bowl, run a film of oil over the top, cover with plastic wrap and refrigerate until you're in the mood for an effortless pasta supper, or a baked potato dressed to the nines. If you are cutting calories, you might try it on steamed spaghetti squash or chilled cucumber "noodles," made from large seedless cucumbers, cut lengthwise into ⅛-inch-thick "noodles," about ½-inch wide.

Serves 8 moderately; 4 Serendipitously.

* Multicolored pasta is available at Grace's Marketplace, 1237 Third Avenue, New York, NY.

Serious Food

(*continued from page 92*)
"Polly wanna party! Polly wanna party!"

Polly got one. She was slapped between the covers of a book named *Green Lights Are Blue* by her author, Ursule Molinero, and became Mondrian, the book's first-person narrator. She was the honored guest in the first of a long series of book-signing parties. The book's title inspired a green-and-blue 13-layer cake and blue mint juleps with sprigs of green mint for garnish. This early success with dyes was to stand Serendipity in good stead at some of their most flamboyant extravaganzas.

Calvin, Patch, and Stephen were born party-givers as others are born artists. They loved organizing them, and had a better time at them than any of their guests. The party they catered for Bobby Short at Carnegie Hall was an example. There were foot-long hot dogs smothered in chili, and gallons of champagne bubbling in cerulean blue long-stemmed glasses. Patch served his Aunt Buba's Jello cake heaped with chocolate ice cream. And Calvin performed his famous chortle, a cross between a chuckle and a snort.

Calvin gave himself and several hundred of his closest friends a New Year's Day celebration that needed only a couple of magnolia trees to bring back the days of the antebellum South. It was held in his loft on Canal Street, empty but for an antique black iron stove and Southern mammy look-alike, red taffeta petticoat intact. When she opened the oven door, out came a roast suckling pig, collard greens, and black-eyed peas. This plus a bowl of eggnog was practically a guarantee that all the abundance that had "gone with the wind" when Tara was sacked would return in 1965.

The 1960s were more party than show. Attendance was by invitation and all the doyens of the fashion press as well as the Serendipity regulars clawed their way in. Though accustomed to plush cushions, they gladly sat on hard wooden bleachers to sip lethal Lady Mendl's Punch, a deceptively fruity concoction liberally laced with vodka and blended with ice. After the third refill, glasses crashed to the white tile floor. Calvin, pince-nez held aloft, was commentator, "and what a commentator," says Bobby Short. "What to wear for a climb up the corporate ladder," he pontificated, and out stepped a corps of Twiggylike nymphets, teenage sprigs led by Lynn Dubal, exposing "see- through" clothes by Stephen Bruce that promised to be very distracting to the corporate eye. Stephen brought new meaning to mad, mod, and mini. His interpretations landed easily on the covers of *Vogue* and *Bazaar*. To add excitement, many were done in prints by Andy

Warhol, all of them snack-centered: The Ice Cream Cone, Pretzel, and the Peppermint Twist.

Calvin Holt's ability to command center stage is no accident. He is a trained professional, a graduate of the Goodman Memorial Theater in Chicago. His classmate and lifelong friend was Geraldine Page, for whom he gave many Serendipity parties. He played summer stock and the borscht circuit with Neil Simon, Herbert Ross, Sid Caesar, and Imogene Coca.

In the films *Loving, The Possession of Joel Delaney*, and *The Secret Garden of Stanley Sweetheart*, he played the lead. After only a brief apprenticeship with José Limon, he danced the lead part in *To Catch a Star* on Broadway.

Thus, improvising came naturally to him. He thinks every creative act is a derivative of a derivative. "Never be intimidated by authority," he says. "No one knows more than you do. There are no rules. Even the experts disagree."

He and Patch were a well-matched pair of collaborators. Patch wrote song lyrics to original music à la Cole Porter for rising stars in such popular new-talent spots of the day as Le Ruban Bleu and Julius Monk's Upstairs at the Downstairs. Calvin took a total immersion course in piano, never having played before, and became Patch's accompanist. Together, they performed at a "decital"* (Patch's word) held in Serendipity's back room, for a select audience of invited guests. It is still the talk of those who attended.

Together, they co-authored a macrobiotic cookbook, *Brown Rice with Love*. It became the basis for a macrobiotic restaurant on Serendipity's second floor. One of its best dishes still survives on the menu. It is Zen Hash.

"Improv" was also the secret of Calvin's gift for romancing the stove. An avid disciple of James Beard, he somehow made each dish his own, adding or subtracting as the spirit moved him, and coming up with a totally original result.

Lynn Dubal, who remains the muse of Serendipity to this day, gave herself a kosher wedding reception, complete with a beflowered *chuppah*, "kosher" ham, and a custom-designed wedding dress and headpiece, a wedding gift from Stephen. Serendipity was closed for the occasion. Ohio wedding guests were open-mouthed in astonishment. They had never seen or imagined anything like Serendipity.

After thirty-six years of parties, it's hard to pick favorites. There were Sweet Sixteen parties, birthday parties, terribly social charity parties, book-signing

---

* A little less than a recital.

parties for luminaries like Anita Loos, Catherine Millinaire, and Peter Beard. There was an all-chocolate party to launch *Chocolatier* magazine and a full-course ginger-flavored party to promote ginger beer for every use other than the standard thirst-quenching one.

Of all the fantastic Serendipity galas, there was one standout. The Blue Denim Party was to Serendipity what the Fourth of July is to the rest of us—an all-out evocation of what the sixties were all about.

In the summer of '69, Stephen Bruce came down with Woodstock fever, and broke out in a rash of blue cloud T-shirts, hot rock, and denim. Serendipity's upstairs parlor became a denim museum, hung with Calvin Klein's shorts, James Beard's specially created apron, Cher's miniskirt, Billy Baldwin's denim-upholstered chair, rodeo jeans off the back of bronco-buster Larry Mayhem, and even James Dean's jeans, ripped off (*continued on page 118*)

Spiced Chicken Flambé

½ chicken breast, deboned and
  trimmed
Batter of egg, salt, and pepper
½ cup breadcrumbs, seasoned with
  allspice, nutmeg, white pepper,
  pinch of salt
2 tablespoons butter

2 jiggers brandy
Splash of Madeira wine
¾ cup heavy cream, warmed
1 tablespoon finely chopped parsley
1 sprig parsley

1. Between 2 sheets of waxed paper, pound chicken breast with a mallet until it is ⅓-inch thick.

2. Dip chicken in egg batter, then roll in seasoned breadcrumbs.

3. In a skillet, melt the butter and sauté the chicken breast over medium heat, about 5 minutes on each side. Fork test to determine if it is cooked through.

4. Pour brandy over the chicken and ignite. When flame goes out, remove chicken from the pan to a hot serving plate and keep it in a warm place.

5. Add Madeira to the pan and scrape. Reduce heat and add the cream. Stir until thickened and a slightly brownish color. Add chopped parsley and pour over chicken. Garnish with a sprig of parsley and serve to one guest in need of pampering.

Sautéed Chicken Livers

½ pound chicken livers, halved
2 tablespoons butter
2 or 3 sliced fresh mushrooms
1 heaping tablespoon minced onion, or
    bits of ham or truffles

½ cup Madeira wine
3 tablespoons Franco-American Beef
    Gravy
Sprig of fresh parsley

1. Sauté the chicken livers in butter until just about done, but still pink. Remove from pan to hot plate.

2. Add more butter if necessary and sauté the mushrooms and onion (or ham or truffles).

3. Add the Madeira and reduce to a glaze. Then add the gravy and continue cooking until the sauce is quite thick. Pour over the cooked chicken livers and garnish with a sprig of fresh parsley. A tablespoon of chopped parsley may be added to the sauce before it is poured.

Serves 2 moderately, 1 Serendipitously.

On the night before Christmas, every last-minute Santa was stuffed with foot-long hot dogs and sent off with late gifts in bright orange wrappings. The three Serendips took off their "formal" attire, rolled up their shirtsleeves, and said, "Now let's cook up something just for us."

Stuffed Steak

4 filets mignon, each 1 inch thick
1 pound prime ground sirloin
4 tablespoons minced red onion
1 tablespoon chopped parsley

1 heaping teaspoon freshly ground
    black pepper and salt
2 or 3 tablespoons butter

The Gravy:

2 tablespoons butter
1 heaping teaspoon minced red onion
½ cup burgundy wine

½ cup Franco-American Beef Gravy
1 tablespoon chopped parsley

1. Trim each filet of all fat, then slice seven-eighths of the way through its center. Open the filet to form a butterfly and flatten with the palm of the hand.

2. Make a tartare, using enough ground beef per portion to make a big meatball. Combine with an equal quantity of minced onion, 1 tablespoon chopped parsley, a heaping teaspoon of pepper and salt. Form into a patty and place on one half of the filet. Close with the other half and press edges to completely enclose the tartare.

3. Do not begin cooking until the filet has reached room temperature. Sauté stuffed steak on both sides in butter in a very hot pan. Sear, rather than cook it. Tartare should be warm when placed in the filet. Remove from the pan while still very rare.

4. To prepare gravy, add more butter to the pan to sauté a heaping table-spoon of minced onions. When the onion is clear, reduce heat and add the wine. Reduce to a glaze and add the Franco-American Beef Gravy. Simmer until thickened, then add a tablespoon of chopped parsley. Pour over the stuffed steak and garnish with a sprig of fresh parsley.

Serves 4 sumptuously.

Southerners love their ragouts. This one was a Valentine to Calvin from Lady Evelyn Dyson, a green-eyed redhead with a palate of British sterling. It features a chewy, flavorful meat more familiar to the European table than the American one. Once tasted, this situation could be remedied.

Oxtail Ragout

2 oxtails, about 5 pounds, cut into
   2-inch pieces
1/4 cup unbleached, all-purpose flour
3 tablespoons olive oil
3 cups beef stock
1 cup burgundy wine
2 cloves garlic, minced
1 bay leaf
1 teaspoon dried thyme

1/2 teaspoon grated nutmeg
1 teaspoon salt
1 teaspoon freshly ground black pepper
1 clove
2 cups coarsely chopped yellow onion
1 1/2 cups carrot rounds, 1/8-inch thick
1/2 cup thinly sliced turnip
Chopped fresh parsley for garnish

1. Dredge oxtails with flour until thoroughly coated. Shake off excess.

2. Heat oil in a heavy Dutch oven and brown the oxtails well in several batches, setting each batch aside until all are browned; return all oxtails to pot.

3. Add stock and wine. Stir in garlic, bay leaf, thyme, nutmeg, salt, pepper, and clove. Add vegetables, immersing them well in the liquid.

4. Set Dutch oven over medium heat. Bring to a boil, cover, reduce heat, and simmer for 2 hours, or until oxtails are very tender. Taste and correct seasoning. Skim fat from sauce, garnish with parsley, and serve immediately over rice.

Serves 4 to 6.

Cioppino

This spicy seafood stew swam over from San Francisco in the hip pocket of James Beard.

1 cup chopped green bell pepper
1½ cups chopped onion
½ cup olive oil
2 14-ounce cans Italian tomatoes, plus the juice
3 tablespoons tomato paste
2 cups dry red wine
1½ teaspoons dried basil, crumbled
1½ teaspoons dried oregano, crumbled
1½ teaspoons dried thyme, crumbled
½ bay leaf
2 teaspoons dried hot red pepper flakes, or to taste

1 parsley sprig plus 6 tablespoons minced fresh parsley leaves for garnish
¾ pound (about 18) shrimp
24 hard-shelled clams, cleaned
1½ pounds halibut or cod fillets, cut into 1½-inch pieces
¾ pound sea scallops, halved
Garlic Parmesan toasts as an accompaniment

1. In a kettle, cook the pepper and onion in oil over a moderately low flame, stirring, until the vegetables are softened.

2. Add tomatoes with the juice, tomato paste, wine, basil, oregano, thyme, bay leaf, red pepper flakes, and the parsley sprig. Bring to a boil, stirring, and cook at a bare simmer, covered, stirring occasionally, for 1½ hours.

3. Meanwhile, shell the shrimp, leaving tails and the last joint intact. Cut down the back of each shrimp with a sharp knife to butterfly it, and devein the shrimp.

4. Discard bay leaf and parsley sprig; bring the mixture to a boil.

5. Stir in the clams. Continue boiling, covered. As they open, transfer the clams with tongs to a bowl for 5 to 20 minutes, until the clams have opened. Discard any unopened clams.

6. Season the stew with salt and add shrimp, halibut, and scallops. Reduce heat to a simmer, stirring gently, and continue simmering, covered, for 5 to 7 minutes, until the fish flakes. Stir in the clams gently, sprinkle the cioppino with minced parsley, and serve it with garlic Parmesan toasts.

Serves 6.

Jambalaya à la Julia

This ham-and-rice stew, which has hundreds of variations and millions of devotees is, like Basin Street Blues, associated with the French Creole quarter of New Orleans. Calvin never got there as a boy. Somehow, it was always hog-butchering time or sausage-making time or cotton-picking time. It took Miss Julia to bring New Orleans to Serendipity.

¼ cup salt pork, cut in small cubes
¾ pound chorizos or hot Italian sausages
4 cups minced onion
3 cups minced celery
3 tablespoons minced garlic
4 cups chopped sweet green peppers
1 cup chopped sweet red peppers
2½ to 3 pounds smoked lean ham, in one thick slice
3 bay leaves
3 sprigs fresh thyme or 1 teaspoon dried
1 32-ounce can Italian plum tomatoes

1 cup Italian parsley, minced
Salt and pepper, to taste
Tabasco sauce, to taste
3 cups bottled clam juice
4 cups water
5 cups brown rice
1½ pounds mushrooms, sliced
5 pounds raw shrimp, shelled and deveined
1½ pounds fresh bay scallops
1½ pounds fresh lobster, cut in sections
½ cup sherry or Madeira wine
½ cup red wine

1. In a large kettle or Dutch oven, cook salt pork cubes, stirring often, till rendered of fat.

2. Cut sausages into ½-inch slices and add to the kettle. Cook for 5 to 10 minutes, stirring to keep from sticking. Add onion, cook, stirring continually, till they are wilted. Add the celery, garlic, green and red peppers.

3. Cut the ham into 1-inch cubes and throw them into the kettle. Add bay leaves, thyme, tomatoes, parsley, salt, pepper, and Tabasco sauce.

4. Add 2 cups clam juice and 1 cup water to mixture. Continue cooking, stirring once or twice from the bottom of the kettle, about 10 minutes.

5. Add dry rice and stir gently. Cover and cook about 5 minutes more.

6. Add the remaining clam juice and water, the mushrooms, shrimp, scallops, and lobster. Cook for 15 to 20 minutes more, stirring often from the bottom to prevent scorching. When the rice and seafood are thoroughly cooked, add sherry (or Madeira) and red wine. Do not stir, but let it cook through, simmering until ready to serve. Serve with a bottle of Tabasco.

Serves 24 moderately, 12 magnanimously.

Cousin Daisy's Chicken Divan

1 pound tender, fresh asparagus
4 tablespoons sweet butter
2 tablespoons flour
1 can chicken broth
4 boneless chicken breasts, skinned and
   halved
A few peppercorns

1 onion, halved
5 or 6 parsley sprigs, coarsely chopped
1 carrot, cut in half
½ cup heavy cream, whipped
3 tablespoons very dry sherry
1 cup grated Parmesan cheese

1. Steam the asparagus for 10 minutes, drain and place in the bottom of a buttered casserole.

2. Melt the butter in a saucepan and blend in the flour. Add the chicken broth gradually. Set aside.

3. Boil the chicken breasts in water to which is added a few peppercorns, the onion, parsley, and carrot. Continue to boil until the chicken is tender (approximately 10 to 15 minutes). Remove the chicken from the pot to cool.

4. Carefully slice the chicken into 16 generous slices. Ladle half the sauce over the asparagus in the casserole.

5. Fold the whipped cream into the remainder of the sauce. Add the sherry and grated cheese. Arrange chicken slices over the asparagus and spoon remaining sauce over the chicken. Sprinkle with more cheese.

6. Bake, uncovered, in a 350-degree oven for 30 minutes, or until it is lightly browned. Turkey breast and broccoli spears may be substituted for chicken and asparagus.

Serves 4 generously.

Bride's Steak Au Poivre

1½-inch-thick prime porterhouse,
   about 1½ to 2 pounds
Salt, to taste
2 tablespoons coarsely crushed pepper-
   corns (use mortar and pestle)

¼ pound butter
½ cup heavy cream
¼ cup brandy

1. Salt steak on both sides. Press pepper on both sides as well, to coat it with a thick crust.

2. Melt butter in a heavy, black cast-iron skillet. Put the steak in the skillet and turn the flame up as high as possible. If the butter scorches, reduce the flame slightly. Sear the steak 5 minutes on each side.

3. Pour out the burnt butter and fat and pour heavy cream in the pan. Stir it around to catch the bits of pepper crust which have fallen off the steak. Add a dash of brandy to the sauce and ignite. Stir sauce, serve steak, and pour sauce over the steak.

Serves 2, and serves them well.

Malibar Curry Querzé

2 cups long-grain rice
½ cup olive oil
¼ pound butter
2 pounds beef, cut into 1-inch cubes
4 shallots, finely chopped
3 garlic cloves, minced

4 tablespoons Spice Islands curry
*   powder*
1 can beef bouillon
½ cup black raisins, soaked overnight
*   in water*
½ cup blanched almonds

1. Wash the rice in water for 20 minutes and strain it.

2. Cook it in a large quantity of boiling, salted water for 10 to 20 minutes, or until the grains are soft enough to be crushed between finger and thumb.

3. Drain in colander and rinse in cold water to separate grains.

4. In a heavy casserole, heat the olive oil and butter. Add the cubed meat and brown it slightly. Add the shallots and garlic cloves and simmer over a low heat for 20 minutes until they are golden brown.

5. Add the curry powder, and beef bouillon to cover. Cook over moderate heat, 350 degrees, for 1 hour, or until most of the liquid has evaporated and the meat is tender.

6. Half an hour before the curry is ready, add ½ cup each of raisins and almonds. Bake in a hot oven at 400 degrees, tossing with a fork occasionally, for 30 minutes or until all liquid is absorbed. Serve with chutney and papadums.

Serves 6 to 8.

Devil's Bones

4 teaspoons dry English mustard
1 cup water
8 beef bones from a cooked standing
*   rib roast of beef*

1½ cups breadcrumbs
6 tablespoons Deviled Sauce
8 sprigs watercress

1. Blend mustard and water together.

2. Dip bones into the mixture, covering well, and then dip into the breadcrumbs.

3. Place in a shallow baking pan and broil until brown and hot, turning occasionally, for about 7 minutes.

4. Serve with Deviled Sauce and decorate with watercress.

Serves 4.

Deviled Sauce

2 tablespoons butter
2 onions, finely minced
1/3 cup ketchup
1/4 cup hot sauce
1/3 cup red wine vinegar
1/4 cup sugar
2 tablespoons chili powder

1 heaping teaspoon garlic powder
1 heaping teaspoon freshly ground
   black pepper
1/4 cup water
1 1/2 cups vegetable oil
1 cup sherry
1/2 cup Dijon mustard

1. Melt butter in a heavy skillet, then add onions and let them soften.

2. Add the ketchup, hot sauce, vinegar, sugar, spices, and water.

3. Add the oil, stir and continue cooking over low heat.

4. Add the sherry, simmer for 10 minutes; add the mustard, simmer 5 minutes; stir all ingredients together, simmer 5 minutes and serve.

About 4½–5 cups.

Side Dishes

Coleslaw

½ cup cider vinegar
½ cup sugar
1 heaping teaspoon powdered mustard
1 teaspoon garlic powder
½ teaspoon white pepper
¾ teaspoon freshly ground black
   pepper

¾ teaspoon salt
1 cup mayonnaise
1 head of cabbage, very finely shredded
1 carrot, finely grated

1. In a bowl, whisk together the vinegar, sugar, spices, and combine well.
2. Add mayonnaise to the mixture and continue blending.
3. In a large bowl, combine the cabbage and grated carrot, tossing and making sure carrot is evenly distributed. Pour the spicy dressing over the cabbage-carrot mixture, scraping the dressing bowl. Toss the slaw quickly until it is well coated. Cover and refrigerate until serving time.

NOTE: If this slaw isn't hot enough for you, feel free to make free use of the pepper mill. Achoo.

Serves 6 to 8.

Serendipitous Mashed Potatoes

3 pounds potatoes
4 tablespoons butter
¾ cup milk
¾ cup mayonnaise
1 teaspoon salt

⅓ teaspoon white pepper
⅓ teaspoon freshly ground black
   pepper
1 handful grated cheddar cheese

1. Peel and quarter the potatoes and drop them into a large pot of cold, salted water. Bring to a moderate boil and cook until they are fork-tender. Half an hour should do it. Remove from heat.
2. Transfer to mixing bowl and mash with masher, wooden spoon, or whisk, adding butter and half the milk.
3. Add the mayonnaise and spices and mash some more, until almost smooth.

4. Add cheese and rest of milk. Mash until smooth and fluffy. This is the mashed potatoes "crust" for our Shepherd's Pie (page 81).

Serves 6.

"Butterfly McQueen was the only celebrity I ever asked for an autograph," said Martin Beck, a limber, nattily dressed Southern charmer who dropped his architectural career at Wall Street skyscraper level to clean the sump pump in Serendipity's basement, ring up the cash register, and finally make it to the top as the ne plus ultra of Serendipity hosts. We love Martin for many things: his outrageous wit, indomitable spirit, his pure, chiseled profile and impure mind, his form, face, manly grace, his Vidalia Onion Marmalade.

Unfortunately, Vidalia onions are a sometimes thing, whereas purple onions abound year round, so we've taken a little poetic license.

Purple Onion Marmalade

1½ pounds purple onions,* sliced thin *⅔ cup dry red wine*
½ cup sugar *⅓ cup plus 1 tablespoon red wine*
1 stick (½ cup) unsalted butter *vinegar*
Salt and pepper, to taste *3½ tablespoons grenadine*

1. In a stainless steel or enameled saucepan, cook onions with the sugar and salt and pepper to taste in butter, covered, over moderately low heat, stirring occasionally, for 30 minutes.
2. Add the wine, the vinegar, and the grenadine.
3. Bring the liquid to a boil, and cook the mixture, uncovered, over moderate heat, stirring occasionally, for 30 minutes.
4. Continue cooking over moderately high heat, stirring until it is thick.
5. Transfer the condiment to a serving bowl and serve it hot with game or cold with pâté. Makes about 2 cups. (See footnote, page 56.)

As for La McQueen, she was most gracious: "Why, shore you kin," she consented, opening a purseful of Xeroxed autographs and handing him one.

---

* For Vidalia Onion Marmalade, use white wine and white wine vinegar.

Tomato Chutney

5 pounds ripe tomatoes
2 lemons, sliced thin
5 cups brown sugar
2½ cups cider vinegar
1 tablespoon whole cloves

1 tablespoon allspice
1 stick cinnamon
2 tablespoons preserved ginger,
   slivered
3 cups currants

1. Wash tomatoes in clear water, then scald in boiling water only long enough to remove skin (about ½ minute). Plunge in cold water, peel, core, and quarter.

2. In a large saucepan, place the tomatoes and lemons. Add the sugar, vinegar, and spices, tied in a cheesecloth square. Boil slowly for 2 hours.

3. Add the slivered ginger and currants and boil 1 hour longer, stirring occasionally.

4. Remove spice bag and pour the chutney into sterilized pint-sized jars* and seal while hot.

Makes about 8 pints.

Dirty Rice

4 cups water or chicken stock
2 cups long-grain rice
1 tablespoon salt
8 tablespoons butter
3 scallions, chopped
2 green peppers, chopped

3 cloves garlic, minced fine
1 pound chicken livers, chopped
1 tablespoon Worcestershire sauce
2 tablespoons chopped parsley
Pepper, to taste

1. Bring water or stock to a boil in a heavy pan. Stir in the rice and salt, return to a boil, reduce heat to low, and cover tightly. Let the rice cook for 25 minutes until it is fluffy and dry.

2. Meanwhile, melt butter in a skillet and sauté scallions, green peppers, garlic, and chicken livers. Add Worcestershire sauce and parsley; mix. Turn off heat.

* See page 56 for the source.

3. Uncover rice pan. Add the sautéed chicken liver mixture and stir. Remove pan from heat, cover, and let stand for 5 minutes.

4. Uncover pan, toss rice with a fork, and if it seems a little dry, add 2 or 3 more tablespoons of butter and continue tossing until butter melts.

5. Add freshly ground pepper and serve immediately.

Serves 6 to 8.

Dilly Beans

Arkansas is a state of down-home towns like Rolling Fork, Blue Eye, and Kazoo City. In each, there are members of the Holt clan, churning out dilly beans as they have since the year one.

2 pounds green string beans, trimmed	¼ cup salt
1 teaspoon cayenne pepper	2½ cups vinegar
4 cloves garlic	2½ cups water
4 large dill sprigs	

1. Pack beans, lengthwise, into four hot pint jars,* leaving ¼-inch space on top. To each pint, add ¼ teaspoon cayenne pepper, 1 garlic clove, and 1 dill sprig.

2. Combine remaining ingredients and bring to a boil. Pour, boiling hot, over the beans, leaving ¼-inch on top. Remove air bubbles. Adjust caps. Process for 10 minutes in a bath of boiling water. You'll get a lot of beans for your trouble.

Makes 4 pints.

* See page 56 for source.

Pickled Watermelon Rind

They grow a lot of watermelon down south, so this is a natural, and delicious, by-product.

2 quarts peeled watermelon rind (the rind of one large watermelon), cut into 1-inch pieces
1 tablespoon lime juice

2 cups sugar
1 cup vinegar
1 tablespoon broken stick cinnamon
1½ teaspoons whole cloves

1. Add rind and lime juice to a quart of water and let it stand overnight; drain.
2. Rinse watermelon cubes and cover with water; cook just until the rind is tender and can be pierced with a fork.
3. Meanwhile, in a 6- or 8-quart kettle, mix the sugar, vinegar, cinnamon, and cloves. Simmer 10 minutes, then strain. To the strained syrup, add watermelon rind and simmer until the rind is clear. Fill hot half-pint jars* with the mixture, leaving ½-inch headroom. Process in hot water bath, boiling for about 5 minutes. Seal and store in a cool place.

Makes 5 half-pints.

Peach Pickle

8 cups sugar
2 cups cider vinegar
2 cups water
7 pounds small, firm, unblemished peaches

1 box or jar of whole cloves
2 3-inch cinnamon sticks

1. In an enamel kettle, combine the sugar with the cider vinegar and water and boil the mixture for 5 minutes.
2. Peel the peaches and stud each peach with 5 or 6 whole cloves. Drop each peach into the syrup as soon as it is prepared.

* See page 56 for source.

3. Add the cinnamon sticks to the syrup and cook the peaches slowly until they are tender.

4. Pack the peaches in hot, sterilized quart-sized Triomphe preserving jars.* Fill the jars to overflowing with the syrup, and seal them immediately. Serve with baked ham or roast duck or goose.

Makes about 4 quarts.

Preserved Kumquats

2 quarts kumquats   *5 cups sugar*

1. Remove stems and leaves from kumquats.
2. Wash and drain the fruit and prick each one several times with a darning needle.
3. Put the fruit in a saucepan, cover it with boiling water, and simmer it for about 20 minutes, or until it is tender.
4. Skim kumquats from the water and stir into the water 5 cups of sugar.
5. Boil the syrup for 5 minutes, add kumquats, and cook gently for about 1 hour, or until the fruit is transparent.
6. Let the fruit stand in the syrup overnight to plump.
7. Reheat fruit and syrup to boiling point, skim fruit from syrup, and pack in sterilized jars.†
8. Cook syrup slowly until it is thick, pour it over the kumquats, and seal the jars.
9. Each kumquat can be partially split and stuffed with a maraschino cherry, a blanched almond, or a wedge of peach before the final heating and packing.

Makes about 4 pints.

---

* Triomphe preserving jars from Williams Sonoma, 20 East 60th Street, New York, and in 34 cities east and west of the Rockies.
† See page 56 for source.

114

Jerry Perles's Aunt Lucille's Georgia Corn Pudding

¼ cup chopped green pepper
1 tablespoon chopped onion
2 tablespoons butter
2 cups fresh or canned corn kernels

3 eggs, beaten
1 cup milk
Salt and pepper, to taste

1. Sauté the pepper and onion in a skillet with butter until the onions are transparent.
2. Combine all the ingredients in a mixing bowl and blend well.
3. Transfer to a buttered casserole and bake at 350 degrees for 1 hour to 1½ hours, until it is golden brown.

Serves 8.

Aunt Lucille's Potato Soufflé

6 medium-sized potatoes
1 chicken bouillon cube
½ cup hot milk
4 tablespoons melted butter

1 teaspoon salt
Freshly ground black pepper, to taste
2 eggs, slightly beaten
1 teaspoon paprika

1. Boil potatoes and put them through a ricer, and into a mixing bowl.
2. Dissolve bouillon cube in hot milk in a small bowl, and add the melted butter, salt, and pepper. Whisk until well blended.
3. Add the hot milk mixture to the potatoes and beat thoroughly.
4. Reserve 1½ tablespoons of the beaten egg; add the remainder of the egg to the potatoes and beat again.
5. Transfer potato mixture to a well-greased 9-inch pie plate. Brush top with 1½ teaspoons of beaten egg combined with paprika. Bake in a hot (450-degree) oven until brown. Serve immediately.

Serves 6.

Ratatouille

Gloria Swanson, an insatiable voyager, returned from some exotic port of call to clue Stephen in to her foolproof remedy for Moctezuma's Revenge. "Swallow three cloves of garlic," she advised, "with a glass of cold milk."

For people who'd rather not have their garlic straight, here is a much more palatable alternative. Hot or cold, it's a delicious way to keep Moctezuma and Dracula at bay.

1 Spanish onion, thinly sliced
1/3 cup water
1/3 cup white wine
1 eggplant, cut in 1-inch cubes (white in summer, purple in winter, about 2 pounds)
1 green pepper, sliced in strips
1 red pepper, sliced in strips
2 or 3 zucchini, sliced in 1/2-inch slices

1 16-ounce can whole tomatoes in puree or 3 pounds fresh, ripe tomatoes
2 or 3 cloves garlic, finely minced
1/2 teaspoon oregano
1 teaspoon fresh basil, chopped
1 teaspoon summer savory
1 pound fresh mushrooms, sliced
Juice of 1/2 lemon
Salt and freshly ground pepper, to taste

1. Sauté the onion in water and wine until wilted and the liquid is mostly absorbed. Add the eggplant and peppers and toss quickly. (The eggplant will give off some water, but if it seems dry, you can add more water and wine.)

2. Add the zucchini and sauté a few minutes longer.

3. Add the rest of the ingredients and simmer, covered, for 30 minutes. Remove cover, turn up the heat, and reduce sauce by letting it boil down, approximately 10 minutes more.

This much-loved side dish is usually sopping in olive oil. You'll find the white wine and water a refreshing substitute.

Serves 8.

Bread and Butter

(*continued from page 99*)
at the scene of his fatal car crash by an overzealous fan, and given to Jackie Curtis, the notorious drag queen. Even Gloria Vanderbilt designed a special denim handbag that was mounted, like a bust by Rodin, on a pedestal under glass.

The denim "group exhibition" was a mere backdrop for the main attraction, Stephen's Blue Denim Collection—jackets, jeans, skirts, and etceteras emblazoned with jewels, nailheads, and hand-painted likenesses of screen and rock stars.

The opening party, attended and acclaimed by press from London to Kazoo City to Tokyo, celebrated "blue" all the way. Lady Mendl's Punch was tinted blue, the walls were painted blue with white clouds and a black lady played blues on an upright piano. When Barbra Streisand and Shirley MacLaine opened their mouths to exchange a laugh, they found them to be dyed blue on the inside. Hermione Gingold went into the ladies' room and dropped her false eyelashes. Her mouth had turned blue, too. Cher went a step further. She named her infant son Elijah Blue.

Stephen's blue jean collection made fashion history for all its fun. Bits and pieces of it are in any museum you care to name: the Metropolitan, the Museum of the City of New York, F.I.T., The Brooklyn Museum, and Kent State University. Serendipity wants to thank all those culturally inclined contributors who gave the denims off their backs for the education of future generations.

In their honor, Serendipity has created several totally delicious blue foods: Blue Corn Nachos with Cheddar (page 24); with Goat Cheese (page 25); with Chicken (page 25); Blue Crackling Cornbread Muffins (page 120); Blue Spoon Bread (page 120).

We're not pulling a dye job on you. This time we're true blue, back to nature and the Santa Fe Indians who grew the blue corn which makes the blue cornmeal and the blue corn chips. Don't you love it?

"They brought humor to dinner, pricked pins in our pretensions," said Edith Simpson. Restaurants become passé faster than last year's hemline, but, say René and Ellin Saltzman, "Serendipity never goes out of style. They grow with the times." Amy Greene had Serendipity's first charge account. She believes, "No matter what life brings, they run with it. If you're sad or depressed, the minute you walk in, you feel good again." Halston agreed. "They make everything fun," he said. Bobby Short and Carol Baker were early charge customers who kept their own wine cellar in the Serendipity basement and gave daily lunch parties, "not only for the marvelous, simple farm food, but because there's always madness here."

Calvin, modest as always, can't help but agree. "I can sell *merde*," he says. "Take our cologne, Summer Camp. It smelled like (*continued on page 155*)

Southern Buttermilk Biscuits

2 cups all-purpose flour, plus more as needed
1/4 teaspoon baking soda
1 tablespoon baking powder

1 teaspoon salt
6 tablespoons solid vegetable shortening
3/4 cup buttermilk

1. Sift the dry ingredients into a roomy bowl. Cut in the shortening with a pastry blender or a fork until the mixture has the texture of coarse meal. Add the buttermilk and mix with your hand, lightly but thoroughly. Add a little more flour if the dough is too sticky. Knead for 1 minute. Wrap in wax paper or foil and refrigerate until well chilled, at least 20 minutes.

2. Preheat oven to 450 degrees.

3. Roll dough out 1/2-inch thick on a lightly floured surface. Always roll from the center out for tender, crisp biscuits. Cut the dough into the desired size biscuits.

4. Place the biscuits on a buttered baking sheet and bake until golden brown, about 10 to 20 minutes.

Makes 25 to 30 biscuits.

Variations:

Cheese Biscuits

Work 1/2 cup freshly grated sharp natural cheddar or Parmesan cheese into the dough before rolling it out 1/8-inch thick. Cut into small biscuits and bake in a preheated 375- or 400-degree oven. Serve with salads or for cocktails.

Rosemary Biscuits

Work 1/2 to 1 teaspoon crushed dried rosemary into the dough before rolling it out 1/2-inch thick.

Blue Crackling Cornbread Muffins

Here's how they start the day southwest of the Mississippi.

1 cup blue cornmeal*
1 cup unbleached all-purpose flour
1/3 cup granulated sugar
2 1/2 teaspoons baking powder
1/4 teaspoon salt

1 cup buttermilk
1 cup diced, crisp-cooked bacon
6 tablespoons sweet butter, melted
1 egg, slightly beaten

1. Preheat oven to 400 degrees. Grease 10 medium-sized muffin cups.
2. Stir dry ingredients together in a bowl. Then stir in the buttermilk, bacon, butter, and egg and mix gently.
3. Pour the batter into the prepared muffin cups. Set on the middle rack of the oven, and bake for 25 minutes. Cornbread is done when the edges are slightly golden and a straw inserted in the center comes out clean.

Ten is never enough, but 10 muffins is what you'll get.

Calvin's Aunt Sybil Loreen's Blue Spoon Bread

Spoon bread is not bread at all, but a kind of cornmeal soufflé. What makes this recipe so unexpected is the addition of whole kernels of corn. Aunt Sybil Loreen never heard of blue corn, never having been west of Blue Eye, Arkansas, in her cotton-picking life. It took Calvin, obsessed with the colors blue and yellow, to orchestrate this variation on an old Southern theme.

3 cups milk
1 cup blue cornmeal*
2 tablespoons melted butter
1 teaspoon salt

3 eggs, separated
1/2 cup cooked (or canned) yellow corn
  kernels

1. Preheat oven to 350 degrees and butter a 1 1/2-quart soufflé dish.
2. Scald 3 cups milk. Gradually add 1 cup blue cornmeal.

---

* Blue cornmeal available at Williams Sonoma, 20 East 60th Street, New York City, and other locations east and west of the Rockies.

3. Cook the mixture, stirring, in the top of a double boiler over boiling water for about 5 minutes, or until it is smooth and thick.

4. Cool slightly and add 2 tablespoons of melted butter and 1 teaspoon salt.

5. Beat 3 egg yolks and add to the mixture.

6. Stir in the cooked (or canned) yellow corn kernels.

7. Beat the 3 egg whites until stiff, and fold into mixture.

8. Pour batter into a prepared (buttered) soufflé dish and bake for about 45 minutes, or until golden. Serve at once, with plenty of butter, to 6 cynics who think Southern cooking is hogwash.

Soda Bread

4¾ cups flour
1½ teaspoons salt
1½ teaspoons baking soda
Scant 3 tablespoons butter

About 2 cups buttermilk
¾ cup currants
⅓ cup caraway seeds

1. Preheat oven to 400 degrees.

2. Sift flour with salt and baking soda into a bowl.

3. Rub in butter with fingertips and mix in the buttermilk to make a soft dough.

4. Add the currants and caraway seeds and continue working with fingertips until they are evenly distributed.

5. Turn dough onto a floured board and shape into a large round, about 2 inches thick.

6. Score deeply (about ¾-inch deep) into quarters, place on a floured baking sheet and bake for 25 to 30 minutes or until the bread sounds hollow when tapped with your knuckles.

If desired, you can double this recipe, bake the bread in a loaf pan, and slice the loaf for sandwiches, the way it's done at Serendipity.

Makes 1 loaf, serves 8.

Challah

1½ packages active dry yeast

¾ cup lukewarm water

½ tablespoon granulated sugar

½ tablespoon coarse salt

1½ tablespoons softened butter

2 eggs

2½ to 2¾ cups all-purpose flour

1 egg yolk mixed with 1 teaspoon cold water

Poppy seeds

1. Proof yeast in lukewarm water in a large bowl.
2. Add sugar, salt, butter, eggs, and 1½ cups of the flour, ½ cup at a time.
3. Beat thoroughly with a wooden spoon or with the hands. Gradually add more flour until the dough is very stiff.
4. Turn the dough out onto a board sprinkled with flour and knead until the dough is smooth and elastic. Then place the dough in a very large buttered bowl and turn to cover the entire surface with butter.
5. Cover with a damp towel and let rise in a warm, draft-free kitchen until doubled in bulk, about 1½ to 2 hours.
6. Punch dough down and divide into 3 equal parts. Roll each part into a rope about 1 inch in diameter on a lightly floured board.
7. Braid the 3 ropes together to make a loaf. Place on a buttered baking sheet. Cover and let rise in a warm place until almost doubled in bulk.
8. Brush the top of the loaf with the egg yolk–cold water glaze and sprinkle with poppy seeds. Bake in a preheated 400-degree oven for 35 to 45 minutes, until the challah sounds hollow when tapped with the knuckles and you hear a fiddler on the roof.

Makes 1 loaf, serves 6.

White Bread for Tea Sandwiches

1 cup milk

1 cup hot water

1 to 1½ tablespoons shortening

1 to 1½ tablespoons butter

2 tablespoons sugar

2½ teaspoons salt

1 cake compressed yeast

¼ cup 85-degree water

6½ cups all-purpose flour, sifted

1. Have all ingredients at about 75 degrees. Scald the milk.

2. Add the hot water, shortening, butter, sugar, and salt to the milk. Mix until well combined.

3. In a separate large bowl, crumble the yeast and soak about 10 minutes, or until dissolved, in ¼ cup 85-degree water.

4. When the milk mixture has cooled to 85 degrees, add it to the dissolved yeast. Blend thoroughly.

5. Start stirring the sifted flour into the dissolved yeast mixture with a spoon. Mix in half the required flour, gradually, and beat about 1 minute. Then, as the rest of the flour is added, mix by hand. When the dough begins to leave the sides of the bowl, turn it out onto a lightly floured board. (Allow 1 tablespoon flour for each cup of flour in the recipe.)

6. Cover dough with a cloth and let it rest 10 to 15 minutes. Then knead gently for 10 minutes, until dough becomes smooth, elastic, and satiny.

7. Grease a large bowl evenly, put dough in it, and turn it over so that the entire surface will be lightly greased. Cover with a damp cloth that has been well wrung out, and set dough to rise in a warm place, about 80 degrees. When dough has doubled in bulk, about 2 hours, punch down the dough with a balled hand. Work edges to center and turn bottom to top.

8. Knead for a few minutes more, in the bowl, cover, and let it rise again until it has not quite doubled in bulk.

9. Place dough on the board, shape lightly into a mound, cover with a cloth and allow to rest for 10 minutes.

10. Preheat oven to 450 degrees. Meanwhile, sprinkle a large baking sheet evenly with cornmeal. Turn dough out onto board and shape it into a large, round loaf. Transfer to baking sheet, cover, and let rise until doubled, about 1 hour.

11. Rub risen loaf generously with flour. Slash shallowly across the top with a sharp knife. Set on middle rack of the oven and bake for 15 minutes. Reduce heat to 375 degrees and bake another 30 minutes, or until loaf is well browned and sounds hollow when tapped on the bottom crust. Let it cool.

Makes 1 large, round loaf.

Whole Wheat–Oatmeal Bread

2¼ cups milk
¼ cup butter
1 tablespoon salt
¼ cup firmly packed brown sugar
2½ to 2¾ cups all-purpose flour

2 cups whole wheat flour
2 packages active dry yeast
2 cups uncooked oats
⅔ cup wheat germ

1. Heat milk, butter, salt, and sugar in a saucepan until lukewarm. Pour liquid into a large mixer bowl. Add 1 cup all-purpose flour and 1 cup whole wheat flour. Beat 2 minutes at medium speed of electric mixer. Add remaining whole wheat flour. Beat 2 minutes at medium speed. Add remaining all-purpose flour and yeast. Beat 2 minutes at medium speed. Stir in oats, wheat germ, and enough additional all-purpose flour to make a soft dough.

2. Turn dough onto a floured surface; knead until smooth and elastic (about 10 minutes). Shape dough into a ball. Place in a buttered bowl; lightly grease surface of dough. Cover with a damp towel and let rise in a warm, draft-free place until nearly double in bulk (about 1 hour).

3. Punch dough down. Shape into 2 large loaves. Place in 2 buttered 8-by-4-by-2½-inch loaf pans. Cover and let rise in a warm place until nearly double in bulk.

4. Bake at 375 degrees for 45 minutes. Remove from pans immediately. Cool on wire rack.

Makes 2 loaves, serves 12.

Rapunzel's Christmas Braid

4 to 4½ cups all-purpose flour
1 teaspoon sugar
¼-ounce package fast-acting yeast
1 teaspoon dried rosemary, ground fine in an electric coffee or spice grinder, or in a mortar with a pestle

¼ cup extra-virgin olive oil
¾ cup water
2 cups pimento-stuffed green olives, chopped
Egg wash of 1 large egg beaten with 1 teaspoon cold water

1. In large bowl, stir together 1 cup flour, the sugar, yeast, and rosemary.

2. In a small saucepan, combine the oil and ¾ cup water and heat over moderate flame until a candy thermometer registers 130°F.

3. Add the warm oil to the flour mixture, whisking until it is smooth.

4. Add the olives and enough of the remaining flour, a little at a time, to form a soft dough.

5. Knead the dough by hand on a lightly floured surface for 8 minutes, or with the dough hook attachment of an electric mixer for 4 minutes, using as much of the remaining flour as necessary to keep dough from sticking, and form it into a ball.

6. Put dough in a well-oiled large bowl, and turn to coat all sides with oil. Let it rise, covered with plastic wrap, in a warm place for 45 minutes to 1 hour, until it doubles in bulk.

7. Punch down the dough, divide it into 3 pieces, and roll each piece between the palms of the hands to form 30-inch-long ropes. Taper the ends of each rope.

8. Place ropes side by side close together and, starting at the middle and working toward one of the ends, braid the 3 ropes together, pressing them into a point at the tapered ends. Turn the bread over and braid the ropes from the middle to the other end, pressing the ropes in the same manner.

9. Transfer the bread to a buttered baking sheet and let it rise, covered loosely with plastic wrap, in a warm place for 30 to 45 minutes, or until it is almost double in bulk. In the meantime, preheat the oven to 400 degrees.

10. Brush bread with some of the egg wash, and bake for 30 minutes, or until it sounds hollow when the bottom is tapped. Let it cool on a rack for 30 minutes.

This bread may be made a day in advance and kept wrapped in plastic to retain freshness.

Makes 1 loaf.

Foccacia

2 pounds all-purpose flour	*3 ounces fresh rosemary leaves*
1 ounce salt	*1/2 cup olive oil*
1/2 ounce active dry yeast	*1 ounce balsamic vinegar*
1/2 teaspoon cracked red pepper	*1/2 teaspoon pressed fresh garlic*
1/2 teaspoon sugar	*3 cups water*

Foccacia is excellent as it is, hot from the oven. It also makes an unusual sandwich bread for such simple fillings as proscuitto and cheese. Or it can be served open-face, spread with a generous sprinkling of goat cheese, sun-dried tomatoes, a bit of basil, salt, and freshly ground black pepper to taste and a squeeze of fresh lemon juice, and returned to the oven just long enough for the cheese to melt.

1. Preheat oven to 425 degrees.
2. Oil a large cookie sheet (18-by-24-inches).
3. Mix all the above ingredients in a large bowl, in the order given, working with a wooden spoon and then with the fingertips until all ingredients are well combined.
4. Turn out dough on a floured surface, and, using more flour if necessary to keep dough from sticking to your hands, knead a bit more until dough is pliable.
5. Transfer to cookie sheet. Working with fingertips, flatten dough evenly until it fills the surface of the sheet.
6. Cover the dough with a damp towel, and let rise for 30 minutes in a warm kitchen.
7. Brush the foccacia with olive oil and bake it until it is golden brown, about 30 minutes.

Makes 1 loaf, serves 6.

Mario's Wife's Grandmother's Easter Egg Bread

There are so many ways to make this bread that we couldn't decide, until a favorite art director friend Mario Cardillo made us an offer we couldn't refuse: an authentic family recipe from Bari, Italy.

2¼ to 3¼ cups unsifted flour
¼ cup sugar
1 teaspoon salt
1 package active dry yeast
⅔ cup milk
2 tablespoons butter
2 eggs, at room temperature
½ cup golden raisins or mixed, candied fruit

¼ cup slivered almonds
½ teaspoon anise seed
2 tablespoons melted butter
6 raw eggs (dyed orange and pink)
Confectioners' sugar icing
Old-fashioned, multicolored rock sugar crystals

1. In a large bowl, thoroughly mix 1 cup flour, sugar, salt, and undissolved yeast.

2. Combine milk and 2 tablespoons butter in a saucepan. Heat over low flame until liquid is warm. Butter does not need to melt.

3. Gradually add second mixture to dry ingredients and beat 2 minutes at medium speed of electric mixer, scraping bowl occasionally.

4. Add 2 eggs and ½ cup flour, or enough flour to make a thick batter.

5. Beat at high speed 2 minutes, scraping bowl occasionally.

6. Stir in enough additional flour to make a soft dough.

7. Turn out onto lightly floured board, knead until smooth and elastic, about 8 to 10 minutes.

8. Place in greased bowl, turning to grease top. Cover and let rise in warm place, free from draft, until doubled in bulk, about 1 hour.

9. In small bowl, combine raisins, almonds, and anise seed.

10. Punch dough down, turn onto lightly floured board.

11. Knead in the raisin-nut-seed mixture.

12. Divide dough in half. Place both halves on a greased baking sheet.

13. Brush top with melted butter to form a glaze.

14. Dip the 6 raw eggs in Easter egg dye and place 3 colored raw eggs in the center of each half.

15. Cover with a clean cloth and let the breads rise in a warm place, free from draft, until they have doubled in bulk, about 1 hour.

16. Bake both loaves in preheated oven at 350 degrees for about 30 to 35 minutes, or until done.

17. Remove from baking sheet and cool on a wire rack. Frost with confectioners' icing and sprinkle with old-fashioned multicolored rock sugar crystals.

Confectioners' Icing

3 cups confectioners' sugar

1. Add enough water to confectioners' sugar to make it into a dribbling consistency.
2. Dribble on top of the cakes. Then decorate with the rock sugar.

Makes 2 loaves.

Hazelnut Brioche Bread

1½ packages active dry yeast
2 tablespoons granulated sugar
½ cup warm water
1 cup melted butter
1½ teaspoons salt

4 cups all-purpose flour
4 eggs
1 cup sliced hazelnuts, lightly toasted
1 egg yolk mixed with ¼ cup light
cream

1. Combine yeast, sugar, and warm water and allow to proof.
2. Mix the melted butter and salt. Then, in a large bowl, combine flour, eggs, melted butter, yeast mixture, and hazelnuts.
3. Beat with the hand until smooth. Place in a buttered bowl, turning the dough to butter the top surface.
4. Cover with a damp towel and set in a warm, draft-free place to rise until light and doubled in bulk, about 1 to 1½ hours. Punch dough down and shape into 2 loaves.
5. Fit into buttered 8-inch-by-4-inch-by-2-inch loaf pans and let rise again in a warm kitchen until doubled in bulk, about 1 hour. Brush with the egg yolk and cream mixture and bake at 400 degrees for 30 minutes, until the loaves are a rich golden brown and sound hollow when tapped with the knuckles.

Delicious warm with lemon curd, makes wonderful toast, but is easier to slice when cooled on a rack.

Makes 2 loaves, each serves 6 to 8.

Chocolate Bread

What the world needs now is more chocolate. Try this for your morning toast, your lunchbox sandwich, your teatime treat. Ah, well. As Oscar Wilde's mother said, "Sin is the only thing in life worth living for."

1 cup milk
2 tablespoons butter
1/2 cup sugar
1 teaspoon vanilla extract
1 package dry yeast dissolved in 1/4 cup tepid water with 1 tablespoon sugar

2 eggs, beaten
3 1/2 cups all-purpose flour
2/3 cup sifted cocoa
12 ounces Nestle's chocolate morsels
2 tablespoons melted butter
Old-fashioned rock sugar crystals

1. Scald milk, remove from heat and add butter, stirring until it melts. Add sugar and vanilla. When mixture is lukewarm, add the yeast mixture (it should be frothy). Add beaten eggs and stir well.

2. In a large bowl, mix the flour and cocoa. Add the chocolate morsels. Last, add the yeast-and-milk mixture and stir vigorously. Turn out onto a floured board and, while the dough rests, clean and butter the bowl.

3. Knead the dough gently 3 to 5 minutes, adding flour if necessary to yield a smooth dough. Put the dough into the buttered bowl, turning it so that butter covers every surface. Cover with a damp towel and place in a draft-free, warm place until doubled in size, about 2 hours.

4. Punch down and knead again 8 to 10 times.

5. Divide dough in half and place both halves on a greased baking sheet, separated by several inches to allow for rising.

6. Brush tops of each loaf with melted butter to form a glaze. Cover with the damp towel and let rise again, about 45 minutes.

7. Preheat oven to 350 degrees.

8. Gently pat top of loaves with old-fashioned rock sugar crystals and bake for 40 to 45 minutes. Cool 10 minutes on baking sheet. Then remove and cool on a wire cake rack.

Makes 2 loaves.

Monkey Bread

When I covered the Italian couture collections for the *Serendipity Times*, I took a Bellini break in Venice. There I ran into James Beard. Serendipity food swami that he was, he insisted I be a guest at his cooking class that very afternoon at the Gritti Palace. To my everlasting joy, the lesson of the day was monkey bread.

2 packages active dry yeast
1 cup granulated sugar
½ cup warm water (100 to 115 degrees approximately)
2 sticks softened sweet butter
1½ tablespoons salt

1 cup warm milk
3 eggs plus 2 egg yolks
6 to 7 cups all-purpose flour
½ cup brown sugar
½ cup currants, presoaked

1. Combine yeast, white sugar, and water in a large mixing bowl. While this is proofing (watch for mixture to swell and form little surface bubbles), stir 1 stick of butter and the salt into the warm milk. The butter does not need to melt completely.

2. Now add the milk mixture to the yeast mixture.

3. Add the 3 eggs and 2 egg yolks and beat with a wooden spoon or with bare hands to blend thoroughly.

4. Add flour, 1 cup at a time, stirring well after each addition. After the first 5 cups, it will get harder to do, and the dough will be sticky.

5. Turn out onto a floured board, and, using a baker's scraper or large spatula, scrape under the flour on the board, lift the dough, and fold it over. Continue to lift and fold, adding more flour to board, until dough is no longer sticky and can be kneaded with your hands. Knead 10 minutes more, until dough is elastic and pliable.

6. Shape dough into a ball and put into a buttered bowl, turning to coat all over with butter. Cover with plastic wrap and set in a warm, draft-free place to rise and double in bulk. Punch the dough down and let it rest for 5 minutes.

7. Turn out onto a lightly floured board, using 1 tablespoon flour, and again shape into a ball. Let it rest for 5 or 10 minutes more. Meanwhile, butter a 10-inch tube pan.

8. In a saucepan, melt the second stick of sweet butter with the brown sugar and currants and mix well.

9. Pinch off enough dough to make golf ball–sized balls. Roll each of the balls in the warm butter mixture and line the bottom of the tube pan with them. Continue to arrange balls in loose layers. Pour what is left of the butter mixture over the top.

10. Cover loosely with foil and let the dough rise to the top of the pan. Bake in a preheated 375-degree oven for about 1 hour. It may take a minute or two more. Tap the top. The bread will sound hollow when ready. If the top browns a little too much, don't worry. It will be served inverted. Unmold and let cool thoroughly before serving, or serve warm, for breakfast, and pull apart.

The only riddle is the name. Nobody knows the answer to that. If you give it as a gift, it won't make a monkey of you. It's a bit of trouble, but it looks and tastes as if it came from the heart.

Makes 1 loaf.

Cakes and Pies

Stuffed Cake

Most of us don't bake cakes unless it's to honor a big event. On larger-than-life occasions, cakes are sometimes stuffed with more than dough.

At bachelor dinners, in the days before women's lib, cakes were sometimes stuffed with chorus girls in G-strings.

In England, Jeremy Burrell almost choked on a "lucky" paper-wrapped sixpence his mother had stuffed into a seed cake for Boxing Day. But along came a big box from J. Arthur Rank.

On Twelfth Night, at the start of Carnival in New Orleans, a regal king's cake is stuffed with a single bean or pecan half; whoever gets it in his portion is declared King or Queen of the Twelfth Night celebration.

An underpaid newlywed, a junior in the diplomatic service, was assigned to his first post in Mexico City. In a de Maupassant twist of fate, he and his bride were invited, by the ambassador, to a lavish dinner party. When the cake was served, the hostess announced that a tiny porcelain doll had been baked inside; the guest who found this morsel in his piece of cake would be obliged to give the next banquet. The wife noticed that her husband had turned deathly pale, and could no longer speak, eat, or drink. He signaled his distress and she understood that the doll was in his mouth. She also was aware that there was no way they could afford to reciprocate on so grand a scale. She laid the blame on Montezuma, and they departed early, leaving the baffled hostess to wonder who had swallowed her doll.

Blackout Cake

When Mia Farrow decided to bake her favorite cake, she asked Serendipity for a recipe for their Blackout Cake. They went overboard and gave her a recipe for, not one, but three Blackout Cakes. The iron butterfly girded herself and went to work with a vengeance. You won't have to work so hard. We've reduced the restaurant recipe to single-cake proportions.

1 pound Baker's unsweetened chocolate
2 pounds brown sugar
1 pound sweet butter
3⅓ cups cake flour
2 heaping tablespoons baking soda
6 eggs
1⅔ tablespoons vanilla

3 cups water
10⅔ ounces sour cream
Blackout Frosting topped with
    Chocolate-Covered Cherries (recipes
    follow)

1. In a double boiler, melt the chocolate and let it cool.

2. Beat the sugar and butter in a mixing bowl with a wire whisk until they are blended and the consistency of mayonnaise.

3. In a second bowl, sift the flour and baking soda and whisk together.

4. In a third bowl, mix the eggs and vanilla and beat well. Add them and the melted chocolate to the sugar-and-butter mixture and blend.

5. Boil water, preheat oven to 350 degrees, and grease three 9-inch layer cake pans.

6. Add one-half of the flour mixture to the batter, blend well, then add the sour cream and beat until well combined.

7. Add the rest of the flour, beat until well blended. Add the 3 cups of boiling water, all at once, and, with a wire whisk, beat until perfectly blended.

8. Line the bottoms of the 3 buttered cake pans with rounds of wax paper or baking paper, butter the rounds, and dust the pans with flour, shaking out the excess. Divide the batter evenly among the pans and bake the layers in the middle of the oven for approximately 30 minutes, or until the sides have pulled away from the pans and a cake tester comes out clean. Let the layers cool in the pans on racks for 10 minutes. Run a thin knife around the edge of each pan, invert onto the racks, and let them cool completely. Then frost with Blackout Frosting, decorate with Chocolate-Covered Cherries, and serve at your own discretion. A dozen dedicated chocolate freaks could overdose on this one.

Blackout Frosting

16 ounces Baker's unsweetened choco-
late
1 cup plus 2½ tablespoons heavy
cream
2⅓ cups white sugar

3 tablespoons Karo syrup
1 tablespoon vanilla
1 cup sour cream
8 ounces Nestle's semisweet chocolate
morsels

1. Melt chocolate over a double boiler and then cool to room temperature.

2. In a pot, bring cream, sugar, and Karo syrup to a boil. Let cool completely.

3. Place the sugar mixture and the melted chocolate in a mixing bowl, and blend. Add the vanilla and sour cream and blend until it is shiny as the crust on chocolate pudding.

4. Frost each layer, and before stacking, sprinkle with ½ cup of chocolate morsels. Stack, frost, and sprinkle with remaining morsels. Then stack and frost the whole cake, top and sides.

Makes frosting for one 3-layer cake.

Chocolate-Covered Cherries

For special birthdays, George Washington's, for instance, go the whole hog before you frost the cake. If the icing gets too hard, beat in 2 tablespoons boiling water, then dip the cherries, stems and all.

1 8-ounce jar maraschino cherries with
stems, drained and rinsed

⅓ cup cherry brandy

1. Arrange the cherries in a small, shallow dish. Pour the brandy over them and let them macerate in the freezer for 30 minutes.

2. Drain the cherries, reserving the brandy for some other use (maybe blending into the icing?), and dip them, stems and all, into the blackout frosting, and let the excess drip off. Arrange the dipped cherries stem end up in a pan lined with wax paper and chill them until it is time to decorate the cake.

135

Summerhouse Cake

For thirty-six years, Serendipity has kept this recipe under wraps. They even hid it from themselves. Fortunately, it just turned up. Old-timers still ask for "that Summerhouse Cake we had for Christmas."

3½ sticks butter
1 pound sugar
1 pound flour, sifted
6 egg yolks, beaten
1½ ounces pure lemon extract (no
    substitutes)

½ cup Kentucky bourbon
6 egg whites, beaten until stiff
1 pound white raisins
1 pound pecan pieces

1. Preheat the oven to 325 degrees. Grease a 10-inch tube pan or two 9-by-5-inch loaf pans.

2. In a large mixing bowl, cream the butter and sugar until light and fluffy. Add 1 cup of flour and continue mixing. Add the beaten egg yolks and 2 more cups of flour.

3. Beat the mixture until it is smooth; then beat in the lemon extract, bourbon, and the remaining flour.

4. Fold in the stiffly beaten egg whites, the raisins, and the pecans.

5. Immediately pour the batter into the prepared cake pan.

6. Place a shallow pan of hot water on the bottom rack of the oven; then place the cake pan on the center rack. Bake 2 hours for the tube cake, 1½ hours for the loaf cakes, or until a cake tester inserted in the cake comes out clean.

7. Let the cake cool in the pan for 20 minutes; then remove the cake from the pan and let cool on a wire rack. Wrap in a triple layer of cheesecloth which has been soaked in bourbon; then wrap tightly in aluminum foil and store in a cool, dry place. Weekly, remove the foil and brush on more bourbon, then rewrap tightly. Indulge, whenever the mood strikes.

Serves 12.

Carrot Bundt Cake

1½ cups butter
2½ cups sugar
4 eggs
1 tablespoon vanilla extract
1 tablespoon cinnamon
½ teaspoon nutmeg
½ teaspoon mace
1 tablespoon grated orange rind
1½ cups pureed, cooked carrots

1½ cups finely chopped black
   walnuts*
1½ cups freshly grated coconut*
3 cups sifted all-purpose flour
1 tablespoon baking soda
1 teaspoon salt
½ cup warm water
¾ cup Frank Cooper's coarse-cut vintage Oxford Marmalade*

1. Preheat the oven to 325 degrees. Grease and flour a 10-inch bundt pan.

2. In a large bowl, cream the butter well, then cream in the sugar until the mixture is very light and fluffy.

3. Add the eggs, one at a time, beating well after each.

4. Stir in vanilla, cinnamon, nutmeg, mace, orange rind, carrots, walnuts, and coconut until all ingredients are well dispersed.

5. Sift the flour, baking soda, and salt together and add, with warm water, to the first mixture. Do not beat when adding the flour mixture, but fold in just until it is well moistened. Finally, gently fold in the marmalade for a marbling effect. Do not overmix at this point, or it might liquefy the jam. Pour the batter into the prepared Bundt pan.

6. Set on the middle rack of the oven and bake for 50 to 60 minutes, or until the edges shrink away slightly from the sides of the pan, and a tester inserted in the center comes out clean. Cool for ½ hour, then loosen from the sides of the pan and turn out on a cake rack. "Aging" for a day or two enhances the flavor. Serve it *au naturel* to 12 sinners for sumptuous teas or seductive breakfast toast. As for the icing, sin and repent.

* Black walnuts, freshly grated coconut, and Cooper's Vintage Oxford Marmalade are available at Dean & Deluca, 560 Broadway, New York City.

Caramel Icing with Chopped Black Walnuts

2⅓ cups brown sugar
1 cup plus 2½ tablespoons heavy
  cream

4½ tablespoons butter
1½ teaspoons vanilla
Black walnuts, chopped fine

1. Cover and cook sugar and cream for about 3 minutes or until steam has washed down any crystals which may have formed on sides of pan.

2. Uncover and cook without stirring to 240 degrees. Add the butter, remove from the heat and cool to 110 degrees.

3. Add the vanilla, and beat the icing until it is thick and creamy. If it becomes too heavy, thin it with a little cream until it is of the right consistency to be spread.

4. Spread over the top and sides of the carrot cake, if you dare, and top with a sprinkling of finely chopped black walnuts.

Makes about 2 cups.

Angel Food Birthday Cake

1½ cups sifted sugar
1 cup cake flour, sifted
½ teaspoon salt
10 egg whites
1 tablespoon water
1 tablespoon lemon juice

1 teaspoon cream of tartar
½ teaspoon vanilla
½ teaspoon almond extract
Enough red food coloring to make the
  cake pink
Orange Glaze (recipe follows)

1. Sift the sugar twice.

2. Resift the flour 3 times with ½ cup of sifted sugar and ½ teaspoon salt.

3. Whip until foamy 10 egg whites, 1 tablespoon water, and 1 tablespoon lemon juice.

4. Add 1 teaspoon cream of tartar to the egg whites.

5. Whip the egg whites until stiff but not dry. Gradually, whip in 1 cup of sifted sugar, 1 teaspoonful at a time.

6. Fold in the vanilla, the almond extract, and the red food coloring.

7. Sift about ¼ cup of the sugar-and-flour mixture over the batter. Fold it gently and briefly. Continue to do this until the mixture is all used up.

8. Pour the batter into an ungreased nonstick 9-inch tube pan. Bake in a preheated oven at 425 degrees for 30 minutes. When removed from oven, invert and let stand for 1½ hours to cool. Remove from pan.

Orange Glaze:

4 cups sugar   2 quarts orange juice
2 tablespoons cornstarch

1. Sift together the sugar and the cornstarch.
2. Add the orange juice to the mixture, blend it with a whisk, and heat in a saucepan over a low flame, stirring to keep from burning, until it has a syrupy consistency.
3. Pour over the pink angel food cake. Use pink candles.

Serves 12.

Cheesecake

The Crust:

4 cups ground walnuts   1 cup salted butter, cut in pieces and
1½ cups cake flour   melted

The Filling:

3 pounds cream cheese at room tem-   3 tablespoons vanilla
   perature   3 cups sour cream
3 cups white sugar   ½ cup lemon juice
9 eggs at room temperature

1. Place all crust ingredients in a large mixing bowl and beat until well blended and mixture resembles coarse meal.
2. Butter a round springform pan 12 inches in diameter. With fingertips, work mixture into the bottom and sides of pan as evenly as possible, using entire mixture.
3. Prepare filling. In a large bowl, beat together cream cheese and sugar until mixture is really soft.

4. Add eggs and vanilla and continue beating. Add the sour cream, a cup at a time, beating thoroughly between each addition. Finally, when the texture is smooth, whisk in the lemon juice.

5. Fill a shallow pan with boiling water and place on the bottom of the oven to humidify the air and keep the cake from cracking.

6. Pour batter over the crust and into the prepared, buttered pan.

7. Bake at 300 degrees for 1 hour; turn off the oven and let cake set in the oven for 1 hour. Cool at room temperature, wrap in plastic, and refrigerate until ready to serve.

Serves 12.

La Rose's Double Rum Cake

1 cup butter
1½ cups honey
6 eggs
Juice and grated rind of 1 orange
1 teaspoon fresh ginger, grated
¾ cup Swans Down cake flour

½ cup cornmeal
2 teaspoons baking powder
1 package Cadbury's Dark Delight
   chocolate (½ pound)
6 tablespoons St. James rum
Hot Rum Sauce (step 8 below)

1. In a large mixing bowl, place the butter and 1 cup of honey and beat with a balloon whisk until it is the consistency of mayonnaise.

2. In a small bowl, beat 6 eggs together gently and add to the first mixture. Continue beating until well combined.

3. In a small bowl, place the orange juice and grated rind and the grated fresh ginger. Mix together well and add to the butter-honey-and-egg mixture. Beat some more.

4. Sift the flour and the cornmeal with the baking powder and add to the mixture. Fluff gently until you have a smooth batter and all the ingredients are thoroughly blended.

5. Grate half of the Cadbury's dark chocolate very fine, and add it to the batter along with 4 tablespoons of rum. Blend well.

6. Pour batter into a generously buttered lasagne-sized baking dish and bake for 1 hour in a preheated 350-degree oven.

7. Grate the remaining half of the Cadbury's chocolate and sprinkle it over

the top of the cake when it comes out of the oven. Place the cake under the broiler for 2 minutes at 500 degrees to melt the chocolate. While the chocolate is soft, you might sculpt someone's name in it, and let it harden.

8. Cool the cake in the pan. Meanwhile, just before serving, heat ½ cup of honey in ½ cup of water with 2 tablespoons of St. James rum, and whisk well. Spoon 1 tablespoon of this hot rum sauce over each piece of cake as you serve it. Or, pour the rum sauce over the entire cake if you prefer.

Makes 1 cake, serves 8.

Famous Chocolate Wafer Log

The busiest yuppie in town can whip up this impressive log in less time than it takes to find a New York taxi during rush hour.

1 cup heavy cream
⅓ cup confectioners' sugar
½ teaspoon vanilla extract

Package of Famous Chocolate Wafer
  Cookies
1 can shredded coconut

1. Whip cream with sugar and vanilla.
2. Reserve 1 cup, and spread each wafer with remaining cream, stacking them up in fives on wax paper. Chill 15 to 20 minutes.
3. On a long, narrow serving tray, lay stacks on side, end-to-end, each wafer sandwiched to its neighbors with whipped cream. You will now have one long log.
4. Spread reserved cup of whipped cream over the outside of the log, covering it completely.
5. Sprinkle the covered log with shredded coconut and chill at least 4 hours.
6. Slice diagonally, so you get many layers of chocolate and whipped cream.

Serves 6 to 8.

Chocolate Cake with Cherries Almondine

8 egg yolks
¼ pound sweet butter
Slightly less than 1 cup sugar
Slightly less than ½ pound German's
sweet baking chocolate

1 cup blanched almonds, ground
8 egg whites, well beaten to form peaks
1 #2 can pitted black bing cherries,
drained of juice

1. In a large mixing bowl, beat the yolks, add butter and sugar, and cream well.

2. Add the melted chocolate, ground almonds, and egg whites.

3. Pour into a shallow, buttered, and floured 11-by-14-inch pan. Place pitted cherries on top. Bake at 375 degrees for about 20 minutes. Cool and cut in squares. If you must swear off chocolate, let this be your final indulgence.

Serves 8 to 10.

Pecan Pie

Serendipity pies are legends in their own right. People have broken diets, bail, and matrimonial ties for these pies.

3 eggs
1 cup sugar
1 cup Karo syrup, Blue Label (no
substitutes)

1 cup pecan pieces

1. In a large bowl, beat eggs slightly.

2. Add sugar, mix; add Karo, mix; add pecans; mix.

3. Pour into a 9-inch unbaked pie shell (page 148).

4. Bake at 350 degrees for 30 minutes or until a silver knife comes out clean. Serve with a dollop of whipped cream and don't tell anyone how easy it is.

Serves 6.

Chocolate Pecan Pie

3 eggs
½ cup sugar
½ cup Karo syrup, Blue Label
2 squares melted Baker's chocolate

1 tablespoon flour
1 teaspoon pure vanilla
1 cup pecan pieces

1. In a bowl, beat eggs slightly. Add sugar, mix; add Karo, mix; add chocolate, mix. Add flour and vanilla, mix; add pecans, mix.
2. Pour into a 9-inch unbaked pie shell (page 148) and bake at 350 degrees for 30 minutes, or until a silver knife comes out clean.

Serves 6.

Lemon Icebox Pie

The Crust:

7 double Nabisco Sugar Honey Gra-
  ham crackers
2 tablespoons dark brown sugar

1 teaspoon cinnamon
½ stick butter, melted

The Filling:

1 14-ounce can sweetened condensed
  milk, Borden's or Nestle's
2 egg yolks

Grated rind of 1 lemon
½ cup fresh lemon juice

1. Crush graham crackers, add sugar and cinnamon, and mix well.
2. Add the melted butter and mix thoroughly.
3. With the back of a tablespoon, press mixture into the bottom and sides of a buttered 8-inch pie pan. Do not bake.
4. In a bowl, mix condensed milk with egg yolks and lemon rind.
5. Pour in the lemon juice and stir to a smooth consistency, allowing the

143

juice to "curdle" and "cook" the eggs and milk. Pour into the graham cracker shell and refrigerate.

6. Serve with a smile and a snowfall of whipped cream.

Serves 6.

Miss Milton's Lovely Fudge Pie

This is it, the pie that seduced the most seductive sex goddess of all time, the lovely MM.

1 stick of butter
½ cup sugar
3 egg yolks, slightly beaten
½ cup flour
2 squares melted Baker's chocolate

1 tablespoon vanilla
3 egg whites, beaten stiff
2 tablespoons strawberry preserves
(Wilkins' Little Scarlet)

1. Butter and lightly flour an 8-inch pie pan.
2. In a mixing bowl, cream the butter and sugar. Add egg yolks, flour, chocolate, and vanilla.
3. Fold in the stiffly beaten egg whites.
4. Using one-fourth of the mixture, spread into pan. Spread 2 tablespoons of strawberry preserves on top of this batter in the pan. Cover with remaining batter, being sure to seal in all of the preserves.
5. Bake in 325-degree oven for about 30 minutes. Great care should be taken in the last few minutes of baking not to overbake. Pie should be of a soft but firm consistency. Serve with whipped cream sprinkled with grated orange rind.

Serves 6.

Deep South Black-Bottom Pie

Gingersnap Crust:

1 cup gingersnap (Zuzu) crumbs   *6 tablespoons butter, melted*

The Chocolate Layer:

1 envelope Knox Gelatin
3 tablespoons cold water
1⅓ cups milk
3 egg yolks
⅓ cup sugar

2¼ teaspoons cornstarch
Pinch salt
1½ squares Baker's unsweetened chocolate
¾ teaspoon vanilla

The Rum Layer:

3 egg whites
Pinch of cream of tartar

¼ cup sugar
2½ teaspoons white rum

1. To make crust, crush gingersnaps, add melted butter, and mix well.

2. With the back of a tablespoon, press mixture into the bottom and sides of a buttered 8-inch pie pan. Do not bake. Chill well.

3. Prepare the chocolate layer. In small bowl, sprinkle gelatin on the cold water.

4. In a double boiler, scald the milk.

5. In a bowl, beat the egg yolks slightly; combine the sugar, cornstarch, and salt, and stir into the egg yolks. Slowly stir in the scalded milk. Continue stirring.

6. Return the mixture to the double boiler; cook, stirring over hot, not boiling, water until custard coats spoon.

7. Remove from heat, stir in gelatin until dissolved. Set aside.

8. Melt chocolate in a saucepan. Remove from heat and slowly stir in the vanilla and one-half the custard. Beat smooth with an egg beater. Cool and pour into the chilled crust.

9. In a bowl, beat 3 egg whites with the cream of tartar until it forms peaks. Gradually add ¼ cup sugar, beating until stiff.

10. Carefully fold in the remaining one-half of the custard and white rum. Pour this on top of the chocolate layer—as much as it will hold. (Reserve remaining egg whites.) Chill the pie and pour on the remainder of the egg whites. Serve with whipped cream sprinkled with shaved chocolate.

Serves 6.

Big Apple Pie

The Filling:

4 apples, peeled and cored	3 eggs
1/4 tablespoon lemon juice (fresh)	1 cup sugar
2 cups sour cream	1 tablespoon vanilla

The Topping:

1 1/2 cups coarsely ground walnuts	1/2 cup brown sugar
1/4 cup cake flour	1 egg yolk
1/4 cup soft salt butter	2 tablespoons water
1/2 tablespoon cinnamon	

1. Mix apples and lemon juice to prevent browning. Put the apples into a prepared pie shell (see page 148).
2. In a bowl, blend sour cream, eggs, and sugar, and pour over the apples to completely cover them.
3. Bake in preheated 400-degree oven until pie filling rises and apples brown. Remove from oven. Trim overhang.

Prepare topping:

4. In a mixing bowl, place the walnuts, flour, butter, cinnamon, and brown sugar. Mix well until all ingredients have a crumblike texture and there are no large lumps.
5. Place this crumb topping over the apples.
6. Beat the yolk and water to make an egg wash and brush the crimped rim of the pie crust with the egg wash.
7. Set pie on the middle rack of the oven and bake for 20 to 30 minutes at 350 degrees. Pie is done when juices are bubbling and apples are tender.
8. Serve warm or cool, topped with whipped cream or vanilla ice cream.

Serves 6.

Chocolate Chess Pie

¼ pound sweet butter
6 ounces bitter chocolate
2 cups sugar
4 eggs, lightly beaten

2 cups pecans
Vanilla extract to taste
Brandy to taste

1. Prepare a pie crust (page 148), but do not bake.
2. In a small pot, melt butter and chocolate together.
3. In a mixing bowl, combine sugar with the chocolate mixture and blend.
4. Add eggs to the mixture, blend; add nuts and flavorings and blend some more.
5. Pour mixture into the pie crust and bake in a preheated 325-degree oven for 1 hour.

Serves 6.

Aunt Lucille's Georgia Chess Pie

½ cup butter
¾ cup sugar
4 eggs
½ teaspoon cinnamon
½ teaspoon nutmeg

2 teaspoons vinegar
1 cup dates, chopped
1 cup pecans
½ cup coconut
1 pie crust (page 148)

1. In a mixing bowl, beat the butter, sugar, and eggs until fluffy.
2. Add the spices, vinegar, dates, pecans, and coconut. Blend thoroughly.
3. Pour mixture into an unbaked pie crust and bake in a preheated oven at 425 degrees for about 30 minutes.

Serves 6.

Perfect Pie Crust

2½ cups unbleached all-purpose flour
2 teaspoons granulated sugar
1 teaspoon salt
8 tablespoons (1 stick) sweet butter,
  chilled

6 tablespoons vegetable shortening,
  chilled
5 to 6 tablespoons ice water, as needed

1. Sift flour, sugar, and salt into a mixing bowl. Add chilled butter and shortening. Working quickly and using your fingers or a pastry blender, rub or cut butter and shortening into the dry ingredients until mixture looks like coarse meal.

2. Sprinkle on the ice water, 2 or 3 tablespoons at a time, and toss with a fork. Turn dough out onto a floured wooden board or marble slab. With the heel of your hand, knead dough away from you, ¼ cup at a time. Scrape it all up into a ball and wrap in wax paper. Chill in refrigerator for 2 hours.

3. Roll dough out to ½-inch thickness on a floured surface. Line a 9-inch pie pan with half the dough. Crimp the edges for a single-crust pie.

4. For prebaking, line dough in the pie pan with foil and fill with beans or rice. Bake in 425° oven for 8 minutes, then remove beans and lining. Prick bottom of dough with a fork and return pie pan to oven for about 10 or 12 minutes, or until crust is golden brown.

Makes one 9-inch double crust, or two 9-inch single crusts.

* *Homage to Steinberg*

Frrrrrozen Sweets

The pride of the house is its frozen drinks. Each requires a blender half full of crushed ice, a spirit of adventure, and the variety of delectable concoctions that follow. A word of caution: After your blender has gone into high speed, lift the cover and look inside. If your frozen smush looks more like slush, slowly add more ice. If it's more like an Antarctic iceberg, slowly add more liquid. When it begins to look like a Jacuzzi in there, the blender has done its work, and you get your diploma in frozen drinkmanship.

Frrrozen Pineapple Lime

1 cup pineapple juice *1 tablespoon applesauce*
5 pineapple chunks *1 tablespoon Rose's Lime Juice*

Top with whipped cream and green sugar.

November 1959

1 cup cranberry juice *1 tablespoon whipped cream*
Generous pinch shredded coconut
1 tablespoon coconut snow (ground,
* shredded coconut)*

Top with whipped cream and red sugar.

Trader Wic's

1 cup pineapple juice *1 tablespoon coconut snow*
Generous pinch shredded coconut

Top with whipped cream, yellow sugar.

Trader Wic's #2

1 cup orange juice *1 tablespoon whipped cream*
Generous pinch shredded coconut
1 tablespoon coconut snow (ground,
* shredded coconut)*

Top with whipped cream, orange sugar.

Apricot Smush

1 cup stewed apricots   1 cup apricot nectar

Top with whipped cream, confetti-colored nonpareils, and a maraschino cherry.

Frozen Espresso

1 cup espresso, at room temperature   1 teaspoon sugar
1 teaspoon instant espresso

Top with whipped cream garnished with grated chocolate.

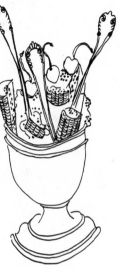

Pink Ice

1½ lemons, peeled and quartered   1 dash red food
1 tablespoon sugar   coloring
                          1 cup water

Top with a red maraschino cherry and lemon peel.

Frozen Tutti Frutti

½ cup pineapple juice   1 tablespoon whipped cream
6 pineapple chunks   3 stemmed cherries
¼ peeled orange   1 tablespoon applesauce

Top with whipped cream with grated orange rind and chopped green maraschino cherries tossed together.

Sweetened Whipped Cream

1 cup heavy cream for whipping   1½ tablespoons corn syrup
1 teaspoon vanilla extract

1. Combine cream and vanilla and mix well.
2. Add the corn syrup slowly, ½ tablespoon at a time, blend, and whip until the cream holds soft peaks.

Serendipity's Best-Kept Secret: The Frozen Hot Chocolate Blend

Our agents have scoured Europe into its darkest chocolate depths. Each of our hand-picked chocolate compositions is, regrettably, a private label. Here are the closest over-the-counter counterparts. We use half dark chocolate, half au lait. Chacun à son gout.

1¹/2 level teaspoons each:	*Callebaut*[1]
sweetened Van Houton cocoa and Droste Cocoa	*Valhrona*[2]
	Lindt
1¹/2 tablespoons sugar	*Cadbury*
1 tablespoon sweet butter	*Anton Berg*[3]
¹/2 cup milk	*Freia*[4]
3 Godiva flowers, dark and light chocolate to taste	*Marabo*[5]
	Girardelli
¹/2 ounce each of the following world-class chocolates:	*Cocoa Barry (solid)*[6]

If you are prepared to go to hell with yourself, add a single Feodora Schokolade[7] and a couple of Ritter Sports.[8]

1. In the top of a double boiler over boiling water, melt the first two cocoas with sugar and butter, creaming to a smooth paste.

2. Add all the remaining chocolates and continue melting, slowly dribbling the milk into the mixture and stirring constantly until thoroughly blended and smooth as silk.

3. Cool to room temperature and follow the recipe for Frozen Hot Chocolate, substituting ¹/2 cup milk for ¹/2 pint milk.

Most of the above ingredients can be found in specialty food stores in America. Also in [1]Belgium, [2]France, [3]Denmark, [4]Norway only, [5]Sweden only, [6]France, [7] and [8] Germany.

Frozen Hot Chocolate

This is the drink almost as famous as Serendipity itself. It has appeared in best-sellers, in the movies, in people's dreams.

1 generous ladleful of Serendipity's se-cret blend of over a dozen imported chocolates

¹/₂ pint milk
¹/₂ quart crushed ice

1. In a quart-sized blender, place all the ingredients, if you can get them. Proceed according to instructions on page 150 under Frrrrrozen Sweets. When a thick stage is reached, pour into a grapefruit bowl and top with a mound of whipped cream, sprinkled with grated chocolate. Insert two straws for sipping and serve with an iced teaspoon for devouring.

Serves 1 chocoholic well.

Frozen Mochaccino

1 generous ladleful of Serendipity's se-cret blend of over a dozen imported chocolates
1 splash of piping hot coffee

1 splash of piping hot espresso
¹/₂ pint fresh milk
¹/₂ quart crushed ice

1. Prepare and garnish as in Frozen Hot Chocolate.

Serves 1 mochaholic.

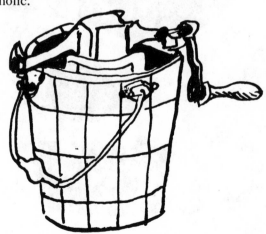

the COOKiE Jar

(continued from page 119)

Chanel Number Two, if you get my drift. But we sold gallons. Amongst ourselves, we called it 'Sucker Camp.' One year we even sold 150 ribbon-tied gift boxes of road apples just to test our strength."

If Rodney Pelter doesn't get their Christmas card every year, he writes them an indignant letter. "It's like being dropped from the 'A' list," he says. The cards, either funky awful or funky hilarious, are the work of theatrical photographer Cris Alexander at his most outrageous.

With a dozen rivals snapping at their heels, Serendipity had to be limber and inventive or the pack would bring it down. In the mid-seventies, they set out to challenge Andy Warhol's *Interview* with a parody called *The Serendipity Times*. It started as a penny-pinching effort to cut the cost of printing new menus. Letting the neighbors pick up the tab and like it seemed a better idea. They sold postage-stamp-sized ads to the shops on the street for $15 each and printed them on the back of the menu as if they were sponsors. The ads grew in size and number. It seemed everyone, even Divine, who bought a personal ad, thought it lent cachet to sponsor Serendipity. Soon there were columns and columnists. Artists and photographers vied with each other to contribute their work at no charge. Antonio, the world-famous fashion illustrator, did a whole issue.

The menu remained as a centerfold, and the *Serendipity Times* expanded to sixteen pages. Much to everybody's amazement, it became the centerpiece for the Rizzoli exhibition that received international hyperbole, "Fashion and Fantasy," an invention of Serendipity's pet "delebrity,"* (continued on page 173)

Aunt Buba's Sand Tarts

2 cups sweet butter, softened
1 tablespoon vanilla
1⅓ cups granulated sugar

6 cups pecans, chopped fine
3⅓ cups cake flour, sifted

1. In a deep bowl, cream the butter with the vanilla and sugar, beating and mashing the mixture against the sides of the bowl with the back of a wooden spoon until it is light and fluffy.

---

* A little less than a celebrity.

2. Now add the pecans and blend well.

3. Stir in the flour mixture by the cupful, continuing the beating and mashing process each time, until it is well incorporated. Continue to beat until the dough is smooth.

4. Cover dough with plastic wrap and refrigerate for at least 3 hours.

5. Shape the cookies on a greased cookie sheet with a paper liner. Take a tablespoon of dough for each and work it flat with your fingertips, to form a round shape approximately 2½ inches in diameter. Then roll cookie into a crescent. Continue shaping and rolling until you've used up all the dough. Chill entire sheet of cookies in the refrigerator, loosely covered in plastic or wax paper, for another 3 hours. (If you don't want to wait another 3 hours plus for sand tarts, this is a good time to slip over to Serendipity.)

6. Preheat oven to 250 degrees and bake your sand tarts for about 1⅓ hours. Rotate the cookie sheet to allow them to bake evenly. Before serving, sprinkle with powdered sugar.

Yield: 36 cookies. (Most important, you made them yourself.)

Golden Tassies
("Miss Milton's Lovely Things")

2 sticks butter　　　　　　　　　　　　*2 cups sifted flour*
2 small packages cream cheese

1. In a deep bowl, cream the butter with the cream cheese, beating and mashing the mixture against the sides of the bowl with the back of a wooden spoon until it is light and fluffy.

2. Add the flour, ½ cup at a time, and work with the fingertips until you have a smooth dough. Chill for 2 or 3 hours.

3. Use little muffin pans or small paper baking shells. Pinch off walnut-sized balls. With thumb, work the pastry to smoothly line the bottom and sides of the container. (This pastry keeps and can be made ahead of time and refrigerated, to be used as needed.)*

---

* Golden tassies may be varied by adding grated orange or lemon rind, spices, ground nuts, chopped cherries—you name it.

Makes about 40 tassies.

Miss Milton's Lovely Fillings
(*for the tassies*)

Jam-Pecan:

Sprinkle chopped pecans in shells. Spoon in strawberry jam. Top with more pecans. Bake 15 to 18 minutes in a 400-degree oven.

Pecan:

Sprinkle chopped pecans into tassie shells, and prepare this mixture:

1 egg
¾ cup light brown sugar (firmly packed)
1 tablespoon melted butter

Pinch of salt
Few drops of vanilla
As many chopped pecans as needed

1. In a bowl, beat the egg and gradually add the sugar, butter, salt, and vanilla, beating well after each addition.
2. Spoon this mixture into the tassies, sprinkle the tops with more chopped pecans, and bake in a 350-degree oven for 15 minutes. Reduce heat to 250 degrees and bake about 10 minutes more.

Makes filling for 18 tassies.

Maid of Honor:

½ cup sugar
1 tablespoon flour
Dash of salt
¾ cup ground, blanched almonds

2 egg yolks, well-beaten
2 tablespoons heavy cream
2 teaspoons grated lemon rind

1. In a bowl, place the sugar, flour, and salt, mixing well. Add the almonds, egg yolks, cream, and lemon rind, mixing well after each addition.

2. Fill tassies not quite full. Bake in a 400-degree oven about 15 to 18 minutes.

Makes filling for 18 tassies.

Mulattoes

2 ounces (2 squares) unsweetened
   chocolate
6 ounces (6 squares) semisweet
   chocolate
2 tablespoons sweet butter
¼ cup sifted all-purpose flour
¼ teaspoon double-acting baking
   powder
⅛ teaspoon salt

2 eggs
¾ cup sugar
2 teaspoons instant coffee
½ teaspoon vanilla extract
6 ounces (1 cup) semisweet chocolate
   morsels
8 ounces (1¼ cups) walnuts or pecans, broken into medium pieces

1. Adjust rack one-third down from top of oven. Preheat to 350 degrees. Cut aluminum foil to fit cookie sheets.

2. In top of a small double boiler over hot water on moderate heat, melt unsweetened and semisweet chocolate with the butter. Stir until smooth. Remove top of double boiler and set aside to cool completely.

3. Sift flour, baking powder, and salt, and set aside. In small bowl of electric mixer, beat eggs, sugar, coffee, and vanilla at high speed for 1 or 2 minutes. On low speed add cooled chocolate, and then the sifted dry ingredients, scraping bowl with rubber spatula as necessary to keep the mixture smooth. Beat only until blended. Stir in the chocolate morsels and nuts.

4. Drop by heaping teaspoonful, 1 inch apart (they hardly spread) on aluminum foil. Slide a cookie tin under the foil.

5. Bake 10 to 12 minutes, reversing the position of the cookie sheet if necessary during baking to insure browning. Tops will be dry and crisp. Centers should remain soft and chewy. Do not overbake. With a wide metal spatula, remove the cookies to cool on a rack. It is best to let them stand, or chill in refrigerator, until the chocolate morsels reharden before serving.

Makes about 30 mulattoes.

The Best Gingerbread Men, Bar None

*¾ cup (1½ sticks) unsalted butter, at
  room temperature*
1 cup packed dark brown sugar
¼ cup molasses
1 egg
2¼ cups unbleached all-purpose flour
2 teaspoons ground ginger

2 teaspoons baking soda
½ teaspoon salt
*1½ teaspoons finely chopped fresh gin-
  ger root*
*½ cup finely chopped crystallized
  ginger*

1. Cream the butter and brown sugar in a large mixer bowl. Beat in the molasses and then the egg.

2. Sift the flour, ground ginger, baking soda, and salt together and stir into the butter mixture with a wooden spoon until blended. Add the fresh and crystallized gingers and stir until well mixed.

3. Refrigerate the dough, covered, at least 2 hours or overnight.

4. Preheat oven to 350 degrees and grease cookie sheets.

5. Roll out dough and cut out the gingerbread men, making sure to dip cookie cutter in flour each time to prevent sticking. Bake 10 minutes till brown.

6. Remove men to wire racks until completely cool.

Makes 3½ to 4 dozen gingerbread men.

Harvey Wallbanger Madeleines

4 eggs
⅔ cup sugar
1 teaspoon Galliano
1 teaspoon finely grated orange rind

1 cup sifted cake flour
*½ cup butter, melted and cooled to
  lukewarm*

1. Prepare buttered shell-shaped madeleine tins and set aside. Preheat oven to 400 degrees.

2. In a bowl, beat the eggs until light and fluffy (10 minutes at high speed on an electric beater). Add the Galliano and orange rind and beat again. Add the sifted flour and continue beating.

3. Fold the lukewarm butter into the mixture. Fill the madeleine tins two-thirds full. Bake for 10 minutes. Turn out on racks.

Makes 24 madeleines.

Chocolate Chip Pizza

2¼ cups all-purpose flour
1 teaspoon baking soda
1 teaspoon salt
1 cup (2 sticks) butter
¾ cup sugar
¾ cup firmly packed brown sugar

1 teaspoon vanilla extract
2 eggs
1 12-ounce package Nestle's semisweet
  chocolate morsels
1 cup chopped nuts

1. Preheat oven to 375 degrees. Butter a 12-inch pizza pan.
2. In a small bowl, combine flour, baking soda, and salt; set aside.
3. In a large mixing bowl, combine butter, white and brown sugar, and vanilla. Beat until creamy.
4. Beat in eggs.
5. Gradually add the flour mixture and beat until smooth.
6. Stir in the chocolate morsels and nuts.
7. Put half the mixture into the prepared pizza pan and bake 20 to 25 minutes, until a straw inserted in the center comes out dry. Cool, remove from pizza pan. Then re-butter pan, fill with remaining half of mixture, and bake as above.

Makes 2 pizzas. Go to your local pizzeria and buy 2 boxes to hold each of the 12-inch pizzas. Slide a chocolate chip pizza in each and give them as gifts to your favorite cookie monster.

Trifles
Treasures
and Temptations

Dark Devil Chocolate Mousse

Eton and Oxford don't give degrees in Advanced Mousse. So a young English viscount transferred to the Serendipity kitchen, where he got a shade too profligate in mixing the fudge pie. Purely by chance, he had created a chocolate mousse intense enough to be rated immoral, illegal, and fattening. With his magna cum laude tucked beneath his arm, he returned to the Mayfair set from whence he came.

1 pound unsweetened baking chocolate
1½ cups heavy cream, heated
4 egg yolks
3 cups sugar

2 tablespoons instant espresso
½ cup boiling water
6 egg whites
¼ teaspoon cream of tartar

1. Melt chocolate in the top of a double boiler over hot, not boiling, water. Place in a mixing bowl. Beat in the heated cream until thoroughly blended.

2. Beat in the egg yolks, one at a time, beating well after each addition. Beat in half the sugar. Dissolve the espresso in boiling water and beat it into the chocolate mixture. Set aside.

3. In another bowl, beat egg whites with cream of tartar until foamy. Slowly beat in the remaining sugar until whites form soft peaks. Fold whites into chocolate mixture gently, until well blended. Chill.

Serve with a wicked wallop of whipped cream to 8 skinnies or 4 Sidney Greenstreets.

Tipsy Trifle

This classic Southern dessert, pretty and sweet, was once "as close as a Southern lady would come to consuming liquor in public—unless she was ill or about to faint."

The Pound Cake:

½ pound butter
1⅔ cups sugar
5 eggs
2 cups cake flour

¼ teaspoon salt
1 tablespoon brandy
1 teaspoon vanilla extract

1. Preheat oven to 300 degrees.
2. Cream butter and sugar together and beat in eggs, one at a time.
3. Beat well. Add flour and salt.
4. Stir in brandy and vanilla; mix thoroughly.
5. Pour into a greased, floured 9-by-5-by-2¾-inch pan.
6. Bake 1½ hours.

The Custard:

1½ quarts milk
1½ cups sugar
5 tablespoons cornstarch

6 eggs
½ cup sherry

1. Pour milk into top of large double boiler (or prepare in 2 batches, if not large enough to hold entire custard).
2. In a mixing bowl, beat together sugar, cornstarch, and eggs until smooth.
3. Add this mixture to the milk and heat until mixture has thickened, stirring constantly. Set aside to cool.
4. Add sherry to cooled custard.

To assemble trifle:

2 cups heavy cream

Raspberry or strawberry preserves

1. Whip cream.
2. Arrange ½-inch cake slices in the bottom of a Waterford crystal serving dish approximately 13-by-9-by-2-inches (any other pan will do, but cut crystal seems the most appropriate).
3. Spread cake slices with preserves, then top with a layer of custard and a layer of whipped cream.
4. Repeat until all ingredients are used—about 3 layers' worth.
5. Chill.
NOTE: For a tipsier trifle, go a little heavier on the brandy and sherry, at your own discretion.

You'll bring more than a trifle of delight to 6 or 8 dinner guests.

Crembalay Julia

Some might deplore her French, but no one could fault her cooking. "I served this dessert every day on Park Avenue before I came to cook for Serendipity," she said in a recent interview.

1⅓ cups heavy cream	*3 egg yolks*
⅔ cup milk	*1 teaspoon vanilla*
¼ cup granulated sugar	*Pint of fresh raspberries*
3 whole eggs	*¾ cup brown sugar*

1. Preheat oven to 300 degrees.

2. Heat cream, milk, and sugar in a heavy saucepan to almost boiling. In a separate bowl beat whole eggs and extra egg yolks together very thoroughly.

3. Gradually add the heated mixture to the eggs, whisking all the while. Return mixture to the saucepan. Cook over moderate heat, stirring constantly with a wooden spoon, until the spoon is coated with the custard (about 4 minutes); remove from the heat. Add the vanilla and mix well.

4. Wash the raspberries well and arrange them in 1 layer at the bottom of a shallow baking dish about 9 inches in diameter. Pour custard into this dish. Set baking dish in a larger pan and place on middle rack of oven. Pour hot water into the outer pan to come level with the custard.

5. Bake for 35 to 45 minutes, until center of custard is set. When done, remove custard from water bath and cool. Cover and chill.

6. A few hours before serving, preheat the broiler. Sift brown sugar evenly over the top of the custard, spreading it to the edges. Set the custard under the broiler as close to the heat as possible. Broil until browned but not burned, about 1½ minutes. Watch closely. Remove and chill.

Miss Julia always served this recipe for 6 Park Avenue ladies' raised pinkies.

Spotted Dick

Mrs. Bridges wasn't the only one who had a monopoly on Cockney cookery. Serendipity had its own resident limey, Jeremy Burrell, who slaved in film production "hitting the gong" for J. Arthur Rank, but he preferred slaving for Serendipity. "The best ten years of my life," he says.

Though his roots were in Yorkshire, he could talk and cook a mean Cockney. Shepherd's Pie, a mainstay of the Serendipity menu, was his contribution. Here is another.

4 ounces flour	*4 ounces red currants (or green citron*
1 teaspoon baking powder	*at Christmas)*
Pinch of salt	*1 ounce golden raisins*
2 ounces sugar	*1 egg*
4 ounces breadcrumbs	*1 tablespoon milk*
2 ounces margarine or suet	

1. Sift together the flour, baking powder, and salt in a large bowl.
2. Add the sugar, breadcrumbs, margarine or finely grated suet, currants (or citron), and raisins. Mix to a stiff dough.
3. Beat the egg with milk in a separate bowl and add to the first mixture, blending thoroughly. If too stiff to mix, add a little water.
4. Butter a 1½-pint pudding basin. This vessel should be narrower at the bottom and wider at the top. Transfer the pudding mixture to the basin. Place a small piece of waxed paper as a cover on top. Over this, place a clean white cloth napkin, secured in place with a string.
5. Bring the 4 corners of the napkin together and tie them in a knot on top of the pudding.
6. Set the pudding basin in a steamer or pot of boiling water ¼-inch deep.
7. Steam for 2 to 2½ hours on top of the stove. Keep checking the water to be sure it has not evaporated.
8. Turn basin upside down on a serving dish. Serve with English treacle or maple syrup, custard, or jam. Jeremy especially recommends rhubarb and ginger jam.

Serves 6 pearlie kings and queens.

Dr. Hopp's Wife's Mother's Norwegian Veiled Peasant Girls

This Norwegian "trifle" offers a charming use of homey, everyday ingredients, and is a pleasantly unexpected way to close a meal.

2 cups Kellogg's corn flakes   *1 cup heavy cream, whipped*
2 cups thick, well-flavored applesauce   *½ cup powdered cocoa, or to taste*

1. Line the bottom of a serving dish with a layer of corn flakes
2. Cover with a layer of applesauce.
3. Top with a layer of whipped cream.
4. Dust with a veil of powdered cocoa.
5. Repeat steps 1 through 4, and start again, repeating the procedure until ingredients are used up, ending with a veil of powdered cocoa.

Serve at once to 6 guests.

Teas and Caffès

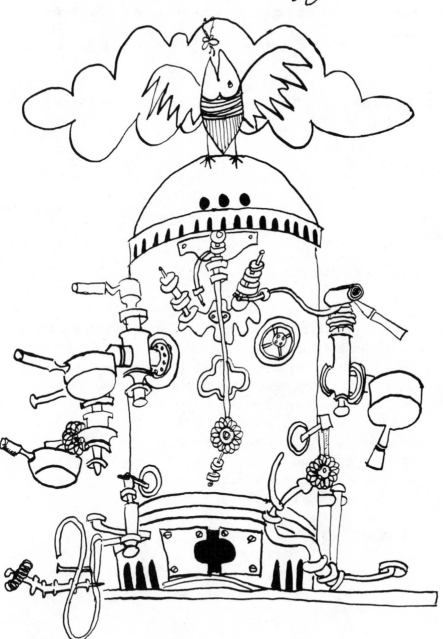

Tea for two or tea for twenty-two, teatime at Serendipity is a combination of four o'clock tea at London's Connaught and a caffè klatsch at Rome's Café Greco. Teas and coffees and a dedicated sweet tooth's assortment of confections abound, including everything you could wish for—and a few you hadn't expected.

Teas

These are the teas on Serendipity's preferred list. They are always freshly brewed to order:

Lapsang Souchong	*Orange and Sweet Spice*
Ceylon with Mint	*Jasmine*
Ceylon	*Gunpowder*
Earl Grey	*Darjeeling*
Oolong	*Sassafras*

Brewing the Perfect Pot of Tea

1. Put a teakettle of cold water on over high heat. Meanwhile, warm the teapot by filling it with hot tap water, letting it stand awhile, and pouring out the water before brewing.

2. Fill a tea ball with tea leaves, allowing 1 teaspoon tea leaves for each cup of water and 1 for the pot. Place in the bottom of the teapot. Pour the boiling water into the teapot. Put the cover on the teapot and cover the pot with a tea "cozy" or heavy cloth to keep it warm. Steep the tea about 5 minutes.

3. Serve with an additional pot of hot water, for guests who prefer weaker tea. Serve with milk, honey, sugar, and lemon slices. A couple of cinnamon sticks, a twist of orange or lemon rind, a few cloves, dry mint leaves, or a splash of sherry could add a dash of *je ne sais quoi* to the pot.

Iced Ginger "Tea"

½ cup thinly sliced peeled fresh ginger-root	*Lemon slices and mint sprigs for garnish*
¼ cup honey, or to taste	

168

1. In a saucepan, combine the gingerroot and the honey with 7 cups water. Bring the liquid to a boil, stirring, and simmer the mixture for 15 minutes.

2. Strain the mixture into a pitcher and chill the "tea" for 30 minutes, or until it is cold. (The ginger tea may be made up to 2 days in advance and kept covered and chilled.)

3. Just before serving, stir in about 2 cups ice cubes and garnish the iced ginger tea with the lemon wedges and the mint sprigs.

Serves 8.

Espresso

Coffeehouses came from Europe and vied with taverns as popular meeting places. Though the founders of the Bank of New York met in a coffeehouse to draw up its charter, the craze took a long coffee break until 1954, the year Serendipity arrived on the scene with its antique "Rube Goldberg" espresso machine exhumed from the Bowery, and put it to work.

Caffè Espresso

Choose your pot and make your espresso: stovetop varieties include the Italian Moka and the French Melior *cafetière* as well as the *café filtre* pot; there is also an ever-increasing selection of small electric espresso machines* to meet the ever-increasing demand. These can make espresso, cappuccino, and brewed American coffee.

The ideal ratio of espresso to water is 2 level tablespoons of freshly ground espresso to 1 cup of water. The steam and boiling water forced through the coffee grounds make the difference.

Tiffany

Fill a cappuccino mug three-fourths full of hot espresso. Top with a heavy shade of whipped cream dusted with green sugar sprinkles.

* Available at Bloomingdale's and W. G. Lemmon, 755 Madison Avenue in New York.

Cinnamon Stick

Full cappuccino mug of hot espresso with a 6-inch cinnamon stick stirrer.

Cappuccino

Fill a mug three-fourths full of milk. Insert steam nozzle to bottom of mug and release steam by turning the steam knob. After a second or so, lower mug so steam nozzle is level with top of liquid. Hold until the milk is whipped to a froth. Return nozzle to bottom of mug and agitate steam from strong to medium until froth is thick and smooth. Shut off steam, allowing milk to settle for a few seconds. Fill cup to brim with hot espresso. Dust with a sprinkling of ground cinnamon.

Chocolaccino

Make cappuccino as directed, and top with a shade of whipped cream and a generous sprinkling of grated bittersweet chocolate.

Nell Gwynne

Make cappuccino as directed, and top with whipped cream, grated orange rind, and bittersweet chocolate shavings.

Serendip

Make cappuccino as directed, and top with whipped cream, grated orange rind, and ground nutmeg.

Kaleidoscope

In oversized mug, make cappuccino as directed, adding a few drops of red food coloring. Insert a large peppermint stick. Top with pink whipped cream and sprinkle with nonpareils. Serve with a miniature kaleidoscope.

Hot Chocolate

In an Irish coffee cup, place a heaping tablespoon of Serendipity's secret blend of over a dozen different imported chocolates.* Moisten with a splash of boiling water. Fill mug with milk and steam as directed for cappuccino. Top with a dollop of whipped cream and sprinkle with fresh grated chocolate, grated orange rind, and cinnamon.

Mochaccino

In an Irish coffee mug, place 1 heaping tablespoon of Serendipity's secret blend of imported chocolates,* a splash of freshly brewed coffee, and a splash of piping hot espresso. Fill the mug with milk and steam as directed for cappuccino. Top with a dollop of whipped cream and shavings of bittersweet chocolate.

* Soon to be available at Serendipity exclusively. If you can't wait, please leave your name with the cashier.

Recipes of the
Famous and Infamous

(*continued from page 155*)

Roberto Polo. He "squeezed out of Rizzoli, as from a ripe fruit, all the juice it had to give"* and spent it on a black-tie dinner dance at El Morocco for fashion freeloaders, trips to Paris for personal wardrobe enhancement, a personal publicist, a complete issueful of ads in *Interview* magazine, and the entire issue of the *Serendipity Times*, which he used as the show's catalogue. Though he left Rizzoli under embarrassing circumstances, we like to think that we exonerated him.

The thing we liked about Roberto was that he didn't do things by halves. What we didn't like so much was that he often paid his chits with rubber checks. He always made good, in time. He went on to bigger things, 110 million dollars bigger. Who knows, he may yet make good this latest tab. Perhaps we haven't "squeezed out, as from a ripe fruit," all the juice that L'Affair Roberto has to give.

Andy Warhol's Tomato Soup

For Andy Warhol, haute cuisine consisted of two dishes: hot fudge sundae and Campbell's tomato soup, which he practically lived on.

1 can Campbell's Tomato Soup   *1 can water from the tap*

Stir soup in saucepan. Slowly stir in 1 can of water. Heat to simmer, stirring occasionally. For cream of tomato soup, prepare as above using milk instead of water.

While Roberto Polo languished in a little provincial jail in Lucca, Italy, he complained bitterly about the "prison cuisine." For a palate cosseted by Maxim's in Paris and Le Cirque and Serendipity in New York, the fare at Lucca was hard to take. His wife, Rosa, was dispatched to Fauchon's in Paris with a grocery list that included white truffles, foie gras, plovers' eggs, beluga caviar (perhaps even nightingales' tongues and ortolans), and a case of Cristal Rosé. To put a point on it, hadn't he more right to wealth, by virtue

* A direct quote from Roberto Polo, appearing in the catalogue accompanying the auction of his collection of eighteenth-century art in Paris before his fall in June 1988.

of his *raffiné* tastes, than his mysterious Mexican victims, rolling in 110 million dollars, who were content to dine in Greek coffee shops?

He thought so. Meanwhile, at Lucca, this is what they expected Roberto the Magnificent, member of the French Legion of Honor, to swallow.

Roberto Polo's Prison Pasta

2 sliced onions
1 clove garlic
4 tablespoons olive oil
1 #2 can tomatoes

1 sprig sweet basil, chopped
½ teaspoon sugar
Salt and pepper, to taste
5 gallons rapidly boiling water

1. Fry onions and garlic in oil, add tomatoes and basil, and cook to a thick sauce.
2. Add sugar, salt, and pepper, stir and simmer 15 minutes.
3. Add 5 gallons of water so it will feed all the inmates.
4. Toss in the pasta, 1 pound for every 4 prisoners, and boil until mushy. If there is not enough water, add more.
NOTE: Don't give them cheese. They don't deserve it.

Zuppa Prigionese
(Roberto Polo's Prison soup)

1 institution-sized pot of briskly boil-
* ing water*
1 dozen fish heads
1 dozen cloves of garlic
Leftovers from inmates' dinner plates
* and other things too disgusting to*
* mention*

Salt and pepper, to taste
Stale bread

Simmer for several hours. Serve piping hot. If they complain, offer them stale bread and water instead. What do they think this is, the Ritz?

Marisol's "Last Supper" Bread

Lorenzo de' Medici had nothing on Roberto Polo as a patron of art. One of Roberto's princely gestures was to bequeath a half-million-dollar Marisol sculpture, *The Last Supper*, to the Metropolitan Museum. There it remains to this day, although since his fall, it has been moved to a less lofty exhibition space. What is probably the world's most expensive loaf of bread was stolen from the *Supper* table, and was replaced by the artist. If your taste in bread is equally epicurean, you might try making it yourself.

1 block of soft wood, like pine	*2 or 3 tablespoons dark walnut floor*
1 whittling knife	*wax*
1 sculptor's rasp	

Shape your bread with knife and rasp. If a dark, shiny crust is desired, wax and buff with walnut-stained floor wax or a maple stain if a golden brown is preferred.

NOTE: Serve only to guests who have the dental equipment of Jaws, the James Bond villain.

When Freddy Suro moved to Paris to become The Honorable Federico Suro Franco, Ambassador, Permanent Delegate of the Dominican Republic to UNESCO at the tender age of thirty, he was the youngest appointed ambassador in the entire diplomatic service. He was also the least affluent. But that didn't stop him from doing his ambassadorial duty and entertaining visitors from abroad, as well as the locals. He even fed and then buried a noted American painter who came for dinner and died of a heart attack just after dessert. And here is the dessert:

The Carmen Miranda

This recipe is so obscene, we can't bring ourselves to print it. If you must have it, may we suggest you write to its author:

The Honorable Federico Suro Franco

c/o Serendipity

A second contribution from the affable Honorable is for a condiment which is passed around all through dinner, but never when Carmen Miranda is being served.

The Rubirosa*

1 wooden peppermill 12 inches long or longer

1 jar, tube, or box of peppercorns, black, green, white, red, rosé,† or mixed to taste

Fill peppermill to the top, screw closed, then twist to pepper your food to taste. Then, as they say in Paris, "Pass the Rubirosa."

Our favorite chocoholics are Baby Jane Holzer, lady of fashion, and her son, Rusty, now a senior at Harvard with a Serendipity charge account of his own. Rusty was weaned on Frozen Hot Chocolate, and mother and son have often sneaked away from a well-balanced dinner prepared by their cook to freak out on a meal of Blackout Cake followed by Frozen Hot Chocolate. For a well-balanced chocolate lunch, followed by a well-balanced chocolate dinner, we offer two choices.

Chocolate Sandwich Rusty Holzer

2 slices white bread, unbuttered
1 Hershey bar with almonds

2 tablespoons sweet butter

Put Hershey bar between 2 slices of bread and brown on both sides in a buttered frying pan. More butter can be added as needed until chocolate is melted.

---

* Porfirio "Rubi" Rubirosa, called the boudoir problem of two continents, was a Dominican diplomat, international playboy, and Casanova whose many conquests included Barbara Hutton and Doris Duke. Though killed in a car crash in Paris in 1965, he is resurrected whenever the dinner party gets dull.
† Rosé peppercorns are available at Zabar's, 2245 Broadway, New York City.

Chocolate Chicken Baby Jane

½ cup plus 1 tablespoon corn oil
2 chickens, 2½ pounds each, quartered
3 rounded tablespoons cocoa
½ teaspoon ground cinnamon
½ teaspoon ground cloves
½ teaspoon anise seed
2 tablespoons sesame seeds
2 cups chicken stock

1 onion, coarsely chopped
3 tomatoes, peeled
1 green pepper, chopped
1 can green chilies
½ cup roasted peanuts, chopped
½ cup roasted almonds, chopped
Salt, sugar, freshly ground pepper, to taste

1. Heat ½ cup oil in a frying pan until hot, and brown chicken on both sides.

2. Meanwhile, put cocoa into a small mixing bowl, add the 1 tablespoon oil, the cinnamon, cloves, anise, and sesame seeds and blend.

3. Place the browned chicken parts in an ovenproof casserole.

4. Pour off oil in skillet and wipe out pan. Pour chicken stock into hot skillet and heat till it sizzles.

5. Add cocoa mixture to skillet and blend it with a whisk.

6. Add onion, tomatoes, green pepper, chilies, peanuts, and almonds to the chocolate sauce.

7. Add salt, pepper, and a touch of sugar to taste.

8. Mix thoroughly over heat and let simmer for 5 minutes.

9. Pour this incredibly rich, spicy chocolate sauce over the chicken, cover the casserole and bake in a preheated oven at 350 degrees until chicken is tender, about 1½ hours.

Serves 8.

In the sixties, you couldn't pick up a copy of *Vogue* that didn't have page after page of pictures of Baby Jane Holzer and her famous tiger's (*continued on page 227*)

Functions Feasts and Follies

A Black Hallowe'en Feast

Count Calvin has an inbred affinity for the Gothic. As writer, producer, director, and lead in the film *Dragula*, he lost more than a pint of blood. To commemorate the eve when all ghouls are out, he invites fellow creatures of the night to partake of a feast in which every bite is black as nevermore, but exotically, erotically, gastronomically beyond compare.

Le Menu Noir

Canapés of Beluga Caviar on Black Pumpernickel
Black Bean Soup
Blackened Standing Rib Roast
Ragout of Black Olives
Pilaf of Wild Thai Rice
Black Seaweed Salad
Blackberry Tart
Four-and-Twenty Blackbirds Baked into a Pie
Black Velvets throughout Dinner   Black Russians with Dessert
Black Turkish Coffee

Beluga Caviar on Black Pumpernickel

1 loaf thinly sliced pumpernickel bread
A bowl of the best beluga over cracked
* ice accompanied by smaller bowls*
* of:*

Chopped, hard-boiled eggs
Finely grated sweet onion
Super-thin, half-slices of lemon
Finely chopped Italian parsley

1. Remove crusts from bread. Cut each slice in thirds and toast lightly.
2. Set out caviar and accompaniments and serve with the toasted pumpernickel, along with Black Velvets. Let guests help themselves from a buffet. Serves any number, depending on the quantity of caviar.

Black Bean Soup

Here is another winner from the land of cotton. It is good, hearty, winter-time food.

2 cups black beans
2 onions, coarsely chopped
1½ pounds of soup beef
2 cups stewed tomatoes
Pinch of thyme

Pinch of parsley
Salt and pepper, to taste
½ cup dry sherry
Sliced lemon
Sliced hard-boiled eggs

1. Soak the beans in water overnight. In the morning, pour off remaining water and add 2½ quarts of boiling water, the onions, stewed tomatoes, soup beef, thyme, parsley, salt, and pepper. Let this cook 5 hours.
2. Then remove the beef, strain the soup, and add the sherry.
3. Serve hot with slices of lemon and hard-boiled egg floating on the surface.

Serves 8 trick-or-treaters.

Blackened Prime Ribs of Beef

1 4-rib standing rib roast, trimmed, weighing 10 to 10½ pounds
2 tablespoons black peppercorns and 1½ bay leaves, crumbled and finely ground together in an electric coffee grinder

2 cloves garlic, finely chopped
2 tablespoons kosher salt
2 medium onions, finely chopped
2 or 3 tablespoons sweet butter, cut into pieces and softened
2 or 3 tablespoons flour

1. Preheat oven to 500 degrees.
2. Place roast, standing on its ribs, in a large roasting pan.
3. Make punctures with a sharp knife through the fat to the meat so the seasoning can be absorbed.
4. In a small bowl, make a paste of the pepper, bay leaves, garlic, salt, onions, butter, and flour.
5. Completely cover the meat and fat with this paste, pressing down with hands.

6. Bake in hot oven for 25 minutes until fat is brown and crisp.

7. Reduce heat to 350 degrees and continue roasting for 1½ hours more, or until a meat thermometer inserted in the fleshy section tells you the roast is rare, about 120 degrees. (Medium rare is 130 degrees, but you must allow for the final "blackening" process on the top of the stove, another 12 minutes of intense heat.)

8. Remove from oven and let stand at room temperature for 15 to 20 minutes.

Blackening the Rib Roast

2 tablespoons kosher salt
2 tablespoons freshly ground white
  pepper
2 tablespoons whole fennel seeds

2½ tablespoons freshly ground black
  pepper
2½ teaspoons dry mustard
2½ teaspoons ground cayenne pepper

1. Combine all the above seasonings in a large bowl and mix well.

2. Lift roast from its pan and roll it, fat side down, in the seasonings, pressing with your hands to be sure every inch of its surface is covered, including the "meat" surface.

3. Heat a very large cast-iron skillet (large enough to hold the roast) for 10 or 12 minutes over high flame until there is white ash in the bottom.

4. Place roast rib side up and fat side down into skillet and continue cooking over very high heat until you've gotten a heavy black crust (about 3 to 4 minutes).

5. Turn the roast and cook all of its surfaces to match the above, 3 to 4 minutes on each surface, including the "meat" side, making sure entire crust is evenly "blackened."

6. Serve while sizzling hot.

NOTE: A commercial hood vent is advised or you may wind up "blackening" yourself and your kitchen. The smoke will be fierce, but we promised you a black feast at all costs, and here it is.

Serves 8 lavishly.

Pilaf of Wild Thai Rice

Wild rice from Thailand is unique in that it is all black. It can be bought only in Oriental markets in your local Chinatown.

1 cup (½ pound) wild Thai rice
5½ cups beef boullion
4 shallots, finely minced
1 clove garlic, finely minced
¼ cup olive oil
1 cup shelled, chopped black walnuts

1 cup black currants
Finely grated rind of 1 large orange
A few minced Chinese water chestnuts
1½ teaspoons salt
Freshly ground black pepper, to taste

1. Put rice in a strainer and run under cold water. Rinse well.
2. Put rice into a medium-sized heavy saucepan, add the boullion, and bring to a rolling boil. Turn heat down to a simmer and cook uncovered for 45 minutes. After ½ hour, check to see if it is done. Rice should not be too soft. Turn rice into a colander and drain.
3. Toss shallots and garlic in a pan with hot olive oil until golden brown; add rice and rest of ingredients. Cook briefly, continually tossing.
4. Adjust seasonings to taste. Let rice stand for a couple of hours to allow flavors to develop. Serve at room temperature.

Serves 6 to 8.

Ragout of Black Olives

This extraordinary recipe comes from the Spain of Hemingway and company. It is a wonderful accompaniment to roast beef, duck, or suckling pig.

3 shallots
A generous lump of butter
2 8-ounce cans Spanish tomato sauce
1 cup dry white wine
2 cubes beef extract
1 tablespoon boiling water

13 ounces spicy black olives, a mixture
  of Kalamata, Nicoise, or other
  Mediterranean-type olives
2 tablespoons olive oil
2 tablespoons capers
8 or 10 slices of black pumpernickel
  bread

1. Peel shallots and chop very fine. Let them simmer to a golden brown in a generous amount of butter—using an enamel pan.

2. Add the tomato sauce, white wine, and beef cubes dissolved in the boiling water. Continue simmering until thick.

3. Meanwhile, pour boiling water over the olives, let stand for a few minutes, drain; then scald again and drain thoroughly.

4. In the meantime, heat another pan with the olive oil. Add the capers, and then the olives. When they have heated through, add them with the oil to the sauce and continue to simmer.

5. Make crisp toast from the bread with crusts removed, and butter it. Put ragout in earthenware casserole and serve with the hot toast.

Serves 8 masked revelers.

"Hijiki" Black Seaweed Salad Akemi

Go to your nearest Japanese grocer for these ingredients.

4 cups black hijiki seaweed
1/2 cup julienned carrots
1/2 cup julienned dried bean curd

1/3 cup soy sauce
1/4 cup granulated sugar

1. Soak the seaweed in salted water for 30 minutes, then drain in a colander.

2. Add the carrots and dried bean curd and stir-fry in vegetable oil.

3. Add soy sauce and sugar to taste.

4. Simmer gently in saucepan over low flame for 30 minutes.

5. Chill and serve.

Serves 6.

Blackberry Tart

The Crust:

1 1/2 cups unbleached flour
2 tablespoons sugar
Pinch of salt
1 teaspoon grated lemon peel

1/4 pound (1 stick) cold unsalted butter
1 egg yolk
5 tablespoons ice water
Softened butter

183

1. For pastry, put dry ingredients and lemon peel in bowl of food processor fitted with metal chopping blade. Process just to mix.

2. Cut butter into small pieces and add to mixture. Process until mixture looks like coarse meal.

3. Add egg yolk and process just until blended.

4. With processor running, quickly add ice water. Process several seconds until pastry forms ball. Stop at once to avoid overmixing.

5. Wrap ball in plastic wrap, chill at least 1 hour.

6. Butter a 10-inch quiche pan with removable bottom. Roll pastry out a little larger than pan. Lift carefully; gently press against bottom and edges.

7. Trim edges; prick bottom and sides with fork and chill 30 minutes.

8. Over pastry, gently press a circle of foil.

9. Fill foil liner with uncooked rice or dried beans to weight it down.

10. Bake pastry in preheated 375-degree oven 15 minutes.

11. Lift out liner with rice or beans (save the ensemble for future pastry baking). Bake crust 5 minutes longer. Cool on rack.

Glaze:

1/2 cup bitter orange marmalade   *2 tablespoons dark rum*

The Filling:

1 envelope softened gelatin   *1 cup sugar*
1/4 cup cold water   *1/2 cup black currant jelly*
3 cups fresh or canned blackberries

1. Heat marmalade and rum over low heat, stirring. Strain.

2. Brush tart shell with 2 tablespoons glaze. Reserve remainder.

3. To prepare blackberry filling, soften gelatin in 1/4 cup cold water.

4. In saucepan, combine blackberries, sugar, and jelly. Cook for 10 minutes over low heat.

5. Cool slightly and stir in the gelatin.

6. Cool thoroughly and pour into the crust.

7. Chill, then brush with remaining orange-rum glaze.

Makes one 10-inch tart.

Four-and-Twenty Blackbirds Baked into a Pie

According to the best Elizabethan authorities, this is how it was done. We'll translate the directions into contemporary English. The rest is up to you.

You must admit, it would be a spectacular finale to the feast.

5 cups flour
Enough water to make dough art
Enough salt to make dough art
A large quantity of beans or rice

1 recipe of pastry for top crust (see
  Perfect Pie Crust, page 148)
24 red-winged blackbirds, the younger
  and smaller, the better

1. In a large mixing bowl, place the flour. Add water and mix till you have a dough. Add salt, ½ cup at a time, and continue mixing until the dough feels gritty to the touch. On a floured surface, roll out to fit the largest pie-shaped aluminum baking pan you can find—12¾-inches in diameter by 4½-inches deep.*

2. Line the pan with the dough art. Cut a hole as big as your fist, or bigger, in the center.

3. Fill the entire "pie shell" with beans or rice to the top, and cover with a "normal" pastry crust. Be sure to cut air vents into this pastry crust (as you might with an apple pie). Crimp the edges and adhere them to the bottom crust.

4. Bake in a 425-degree oven for about 18 or 20 minutes, or until crust is golden brown. Cool in tin to room temperature. When completely cool, carefully lift "pie" from pan (bottom should be hard as a rock) and remove the "filler" (beans or rice) through the hole, being careful not to break top crust. When empty, set on a huge platter.

5. After the feast (including the dessert) has been eaten, and while the Black Russians are being served, fill the empty "pie" shell from the bottom hole with 24 blackbirds, and set it before the guests at once. "Open," or cut a wedge into the pie (very gently, please).

---

* Giant pie pan available at Louis Kaplan, 250 Lafayette Street, New York. See Annette Verona for assistance.

185

"And when the pie is opened, the birds began to sing," we hope. As in the time of Elizabeth I, a royal banquet warrants a flamboyant finale.*

A Thanksgiving Banquet

Cream of Chestnut Soup
A Bird Within a Bird Within a Bird Within a Bird
Fruit and Nut Dressing
Sweet Potato Pie

Sherry Jubilee   *Peach Pickle*
Braised Brussels Sprouts   *Braised Baby Carrots*

White Salad

Cornbread Sticks Dixie   *Herb Butter*

Pecan Pumpkin Pie

A Bird Within a Bird Within a Bird Within a Bird

Calvin Holt, a card-carrying member of the "nothing succeeds like excess" club, claims this creation (and execution) as his four-star television triumph.

1 quail, skinned and boned
1 squab, skinned, boned, and big
* enough to swallow the quail*
1 pheasant, skinned, boned, and big
* enough to swallow the squab*
1 turkey, boned (except for legs and
* wings) but not skinned, and big*
* enough to swallow the pheasant*

Salt and pepper
Butter
2 teaspoons rubbed sage, crushed
2 teaspoons crushed whole rosemary
* leaves*

1. Rinse the quail, squab, pheasant, and turkey inside and out and pat dry with paper towels.
2. Sprinkle the turkey inside and out with salt and pepper. Do the same with the pheasant, squab, and quail.

* "Cutting up the lid of the great Pie, all the Birds will flie out, which is to delight and pleasure shew to the company." This recipe was found in *Epulario, The Italian Banquet*, and translated into contemporary terms with help from Ms. Annette Verona, who could have laughed, but didn't, and came up with the pan and the ingenious suggestion for a dough art crust.

3. Stuff the quail with what it will hold of the fruit and nut dressing (see page 188, or use any stuffing of your choice), and bake the remaining dressing in a casserole at the same time as the stuffed birds.

4. Brush quail all over with butter. Sprinkle with sage and rosemary and pop it into the squab, breast side up.

5. Butter the squab, sprinkle with sage and rosemary and slide it into the pheasant, breast side up.

6. Brush butter over the pheasant, sprinkle with the herbs and stuff it into the turkey, breast side up. Truss the turkey.

7. Use the following directions for roasting a turkey, beginning with step #2. Since your turkey will now weigh more than 12 pounds, check cooking time with your butcher based on its total "stuffed" weight. When bird is roasted, carve on the diagonal for a parquet-like pattern of white against dark meat.

It will serve a small battalion.

Roasting a 12-pound turkey:

*12-pound ready-to-cook turkey,
  deboned*
*Salt and freshly ground pepper, to
  taste*
*Stuffing for a 12-pound bird (see
  Fruit and Nut Dressing, page 188)*

4 tablespoons melted butter
1 teaspoon rubbed sage, crushed
*1 teaspoon crushed whole rosemary
  leaves*
¼ cup cognac

1. Sprinkle the turkey inside and out with salt and pepper.

2. Preheat the oven to 375 degrees.

3. Place the turkey back side down in a roasting pan and brush all over the top and sides with butter. Sprinkle with sage and rosemary.

4. Place the turkey in the oven and bake 30 minutes. Add the cognac to the pan and baste the turkey well. Cover the turkey loosely with a sheet of aluminum foil, and continue baking.

5. Continue roasting the turkey, basting often, about 1 hour. Turn the roasting pan as the turkey cooks, to ensure even browning.

6. When the turkey has cooked for a total of 1½ hours, reduce the oven heat to 350 degrees.

7. After 30 minutes (a total cooking time of 2 hours), reduce the oven heat to 325 degrees. Continue cooking and basting 1½ hours.

8. Untruss turkey. Strain the pan liquid, skimming off and discarding fat as necessary.

9. Let the turkey rest for 30 minutes before carving.

10. Carve the turkey. Serve it with stuffing and hot pan gravy.

It serves 8 serious feeders, 12 dilettantes.

Fruit and Nut Dressing (the best ever)

1 pound cooked, peeled chestnuts (see instructions below)
¾ pound pitted prunes
½ cup dried currants
18 dried apricot halves
Hot tea to cover the 3 dried fruits
⅛ pound lean salt pork*
1 turkey gizzard, trimmed of tough membranes*
1 turkey liver*
⅓ pound equal amounts pork and veal, ground together

¼ cup butter
1 teaspoon ground sage
1 teaspoon rosemary
Salt and freshly ground pepper, to taste
2 pears, peeled, cored, and cut into ¼-inch cubes
3 apples, peeled, cored, and cut into ¼-inch cubes
6 ounces broken pecans and walnuts, toasted
½ cup cognac

1. Cut the cooked and peeled chestnuts into ½-inch cubes. Set aside. (See "How to Peel Chestnuts," page 189.)

2. Place prunes, currants, and apricots in a mixing bowl and add hot tea to cover. Let them soak until ready to use.

3. Heat the butter in a skillet and add the salt pork-gizzard-liver mixture. Cook until it loses its raw red color, and add the veal and pork mixture. Cook, stirring down with the side of a wooden spoon to break up the lumps, until it loses its red color. Sprinkle with sage, rosemary, salt, and pepper.

4. Spoon and scrape the meat mixture into a mixing bowl.

5. Drain the prunes, currants, and apricots. Cut prunes and apricots into small pieces. Add them to the meat mixture. Add the chestnuts, pears,

* Have butcher grind together the salt pork, gizzard, and liver.

apples, pecans, and cognac. Blend well. Add salt and pepper to taste. Set aside until ready to use.

Yield: Stuffing for a 12-pound turkey. Extra stuffing may be baked in a pan with the turkey for about an hour.

How to Peel Chestnuts:

With a sharp paring knife, make an incision around the perimeter of each chestnut, starting and ending on either side of the stem end. Place the chestnuts in one layer in a baking pan just large enough to hold them. Put them in a preheated 450-degree oven and bake about 10 minutes, or until they open. Let the chestnuts cool just until they can be handled. Peel them while they are hot.

Cream of Chestnut Soup Calvin

This isn't just a recipe. This will be his epitaph.

2½ cups chestnuts which have been blanched for 15 minutes, peeled and chopped (set ½-cup aside for garnish)
6 cups chicken stock

1 onion, finely chopped
1 cup chopped celery
2 tablespoons butter
2 cups heavy cream
Salt and pepper, to taste

1. Place chestnuts and chicken stock in a saucepan and bring to a boil. Set aside.
2. Sauté onion and celery in butter until soft but not brown. Add to chicken stock and simmer for 15 minutes.
3. Place the above ingredients in a food processor or blender and process until smooth.
4. Return puree to the saucepan, stir in the 2 cups of heavy cream and simmer for 5 to 10 minutes longer. Season to taste.

5. Serve immediately garnished with a dab of crème fraîche, a sprinkle of ground chestnuts, chopped parsley, and a dash of nutmeg.

Serves 8.

Sweet Potato Pie

1½ cups mashed, cooked yams
Enough fresh orange juice to give yams
the consistency of a thick white sauce
3 eggs
⅓ cup sugar
¼ cup milk
½ teaspoon cinnamon

½ teaspoon ground cloves
Pinch of salt
¼ cup chopped almonds
2 tablespoons melted butter

1. Cook yams in boiling water until tender and mash them; then add orange juice to yams.
2. Beat eggs with sugar until mixture is light. Add milk, cinnamon, ground cloves, and a pinch of salt to egg mixture.
3. Blend egg mixture thoroughly with yam mixture, and pour the filling into a 9-inch pie plate lined with flaky pastry. Sprinkle the top with ¼ cup almonds, finely chopped and tossed in 2 tablespoons melted butter.
4. Bake pie in a very hot, 450-degree oven for 10 minutes; reduce heat to 350 degrees and bake for 30 to 35 minutes longer.

Makes 1 pie.

Flaky Pastry

2 cups sifted flour
1 teaspoon salt

1 cup cold butter
4 to 6 tablespoons ice water

1. Sift flour and salt into a chilled mixing bowl.
2. With 2 knives or a pastry blender, cut in ⅓ cup cold butter until mixture becomes mealy.
3. Cut in another ⅓ cup cold butter, to make lumps the size of small peas.

4. Sprinkle ice water (as little as possible), a tablespoon at a time, over the dough and stir it quickly and gently until it can be gathered together with a fork and cleans the bowl.

5. Form the dough into a ball, wrap in wax paper, chill for half-hour.

6. Roll out the dough into a rectangle about ⅓-inch thick and cover it with the remaining ½ cup cold butter, cut in thin shavings.

7. Fold upper third of the dough over the center and fold the lower third of dough over the upper flap, making 3 layers.

8. Give the dough a quarter turn, roll it out thinly in a rectangle, and fold it again in thirds.

9. Chill the dough for several hours or overnight before dividing it in half to make a 2-crust pie.

Makes pastry for a 2-crust pie.

Sherry Jubilee

1 package black cherry Jell-O
½ cup boiling water

1 #2 can black bing cherries, pitted
½ cup of the best sherry

1. Dissolve Jell-O in ½ cup of boiling water in a bowl.

2. Drain the cherries, retain the juice, and add 1 cup cherry juice to the Jello mixture.

3. Add ½ cup of sherry and all the cherries in the can to the Jell-O mixture.

4. Stir well and pour entire mixture into a mold. Refrigerate until it is chilled and firm.

5. Unmold by immersing mold to rim in a basin of hot water and shaking gently until edges loosen. Place a serving dish over the mold and invert it. Out it will come.

NOTE: It makes a refreshing dessert when served with a bowl of whipped cream.

Serves 8.

Braised Brussels Sprouts

1 pound brussels sprouts
4 tablespoons (½ stick) butter

Salt and pepper, to taste

1. Preheat oven to 350 degrees.
2. Cook brussels sprouts for 5 minutes in a large kettle of boiling, salted water.
3. Drain and put in a heavy covered casserole with butter, salt, and pepper.
4. Cover brussels sprouts with buttered brown paper and put cover on casserole. Bake 20 to 30 minutes until fork tender.

Serves 8.

Braised Baby Carrots

1 pound baby carrots
4 tablespoons (½ stick) butter
Salt, pepper, nutmeg, to taste

Pinch of sugar
½ cup water

1. Scrape and wash carrots.
2. Cook for 3 to 5 minutes in a pot of boiling, salted water.
3. Drain and place in a casserole with the butter, salt, pepper, nutmeg, and sugar. Add water and cover.
4. Cook over low heat about 25 to 30 minutes until liquid has evaporated and carrots are tender.

Serves 8.

White Salad

2 egg whites, stiffly beaten
½ cup sugar
¼ teaspoon salt
1 teaspoon flour
2 tablespoons blueberry vinegar
Juice of 1½ lemons

1 fine, large fresh pineapple, cut in chunks
1 #2 can white pitted cherries
1 cup marshmallows, finely diced
½ cup almonds, finely chopped
1 cup heavy cream, whipped

192

1. In a medium-sized bowl, whip egg whites, sugar, salt, flour, vinegar, and lemon juice together with a wire whisk.

2. Cook the mixture in the top of a double boiler until it is thick.

3. Remove from heat, pour into a bowl, and chill for several hours, or even overnight.

4. Just before serving, add the pineapple, cherries, marshmallows, almonds, and whipped cream. Blend and hold for applause.

This classic Southern salad, almost unknown north of the Mason-Dixon Line, is an inspiration with roast birds.

It will delight 8 Yankees.

Cornbread Sticks Dixie

2 eggs
2 cups buttermilk
3 tablespoons melted butter
2 cups water-ground white cornmeal

3 teaspoons baking powder
1 teaspoon baking soda
1 teaspoon salt

1. Beat eggs and add the buttermilk and melted butter. Set aside.

2. Sift together the cornmeal, baking powder, baking soda, and salt.

3. Stir the dry ingredients into the egg-and-buttermilk mixture.

4. Preheat oven to 450 degrees. Butter a cast-iron corn-stick pan and heat it in the oven. Pour in the batter and bake the cornbread sticks for about 15 minutes. Serve hot, with plenty of butter.

NOTE: Southern cornbread is always made with white cornmeal. It is heresy to use the yellow, to add flour, or to use any sugar. The bread is crumbly, but nutlike and delicious.

Makes about 24 sticks.

Herb Butter

8 tablespoons (1 stick) sweet butter

1 tablespoon finely chopped fresh herb
or mixed herbs of your choice

1. Combine the butter and herb (or mixed herbs) in the bowl of a food processor fitted with a steel blade, and process until smooth.

2. Use a mellon-baller to make perfect balls of butter, and chill until ready to serve.

Makes 16 butter balls.

Pecan Pumpkin Pie

2 cups strained pumpkin
1 cup brown sugar
1½ cups condensed milk
6 eggs, lightly beaten
2 teaspoons cinnamon
2 teaspoons mace

1 teaspoon ground cloves
1 teaspoon ground ginger
¼ teaspoon salt
½ cup chopped pecans
½ recipe for Perfect Pie Crust (see page 148)

1. Combine all the ingredients except pie crust in the order given, in a bowl, and blend.

2. Turn into a prepared crust-lined 9-inch pie pan.

3. Bake in a 375-degree oven for 35 minutes or until the filling is set. Cool on a rack.

Serves 8.

A White Christmas Dinner

Vichyssoise
Blanquette de Veau
Dilled Mashed Potatoes with Crème Fraîche
White Asparagus with Hollandaise Sauce
Endive Salad
White Chocolate Mousse
Taittinger Blanc de Blancs

Vichyssoise

4 russet potatoes, peeled and cut into
  1-inch cubes
The white part of 1 leek, washed well
  and chopped
1 ham hock
5 cups canned chicken broth

1 small bay leaf
2 cups milk, scalded
½ teaspoon salt, or to taste
¼ teaspoon white pepper, or to taste
2 tablespoons snipped fresh chives

1. In a medium-sized heavy saucepan, combine the potatoes, the leek, the ham hock, the chicken broth, and the bay leaf. Bring to a boil, and simmer, covered, for 25 to 30 minutes, or until the potatoes are very soft.

2. Let the mixture cool. Remove the ham hock, reserving it for another use, and the bay leaf, and in a blender, puree the mixture in batches, until it is smooth.

3. In a bowl, combine the puree, the milk, the salt, and the white pepper, and chill the soup, covered, for at least 4 hours and up to 24 hours.

4. Serve in chilled bowls sprinkled with fresh chives.

Serves 8.

Blanquette de Veau

As lily-white and as elegant a main course for a White Christmas dinner as you could wish.

1½ sticks sweet butter
3 pounds veal, cut from a deboned
  loin, in ½-inch cubes
½ cup unbleached, all-purpose flour
1½ teaspoons salt
1½ teaspoons freshly ground black
  pepper
1 scant teaspoon freshly grated nutmeg

1½ pounds white, firm, sliced mushrooms
3 cups coarsely ground yellow onion
2 tablespoons sherry
3 to 4 cups chicken stock
¾ cup heavy cream
Freshly chopped chives for garnish

195

1. Preheat oven to 350 degrees.

2. Melt one stick of butter in a heavy casserole. Add the veal and cook, turning frequently, without browning.

3. Stir 3 tablespoons of flour, salt, pepper, and nutmeg together in a small bowl, and sprinkle over the veal. Continue to cook over low heat, stirring, for 5 minutes. Flour and veal must not be allowed to brown or it will muddy our overall theme.

4. Add mushrooms, onion, sherry, and enough stock just to cover the meat and vegetables. Raise heat to medium, bring to a boil, cover and bake in the oven for 1½ hours.

5. Remove from oven and pour through a strainer over a bowl. Set aside solids and liquid separately.

6. Melt remaining butter in casserole over medium heat. Sprinkle rest of flour in and cook over low heat for 5 minutes, whisking constantly.

7. Whisk reserved cooking liquid slowly into butter-and-flour mixture and bring to a simmer. Cook slowly, stirring constantly, for 5 minutes.

8. Whisk in cream and additional salt, pepper, and nutmeg to taste. Return veal and vegetables to the casserole and simmer together to heat through, about 5 minutes. Transfer to a deep, silver serving dish and garnish with chives.

Serves 8.

Dilled Mashed Potatoes with Crème Fraîche

6 russet potatoes, peeled and halved
4 tablespoons sweet butter
½ cup crème fraîche

6 tablespoons chopped fresh dill
Salt and pepper, to taste
½ cup warm milk

1. Boil the potatoes in rapidly boiling salted water until tender enough to be pierced easily with a fork. Discard water and return potatoes to cooking pot. Turn on heat and let any moisture in potatoes evaporate.

2. Remove potatoes from heat and transfer to a mixing bowl. With hand-held potato masher, wooden spoon, or whisk, mash potatoes well, until smooth.

3. Combine the warm milk and the crème fraîche and fold into the potatoes, continuing to mash. Fold in the dill and blend thoroughly. Add salt,

pepper, and butter to taste, and combine until well blended. Serve while warm.

Serves 8.

White Asparagus with Hollandaise Sauce

Admittedly, not every greengrocer has this delicacy just when you want it. But Grace's Marketplace of 1237 Third Avenue in New York will special order it if you give them a week's notice. They gave me their word.

Two pounds makes six generous portions. Take each stalk by its end and bend it gently. It will snap at the point where the toughness ends. Rinse the tip ends under cold running water. Tie the asparagus into several bunches.

Either steam the asparagus, the bunches standing upright in a small amount of boiling water in an asparagus cooker or deep, covered pot, or cook them in a large pot of boiling, salted water. In any event, be careful not to overcook. You might let one or two stalks hang loose, so you can fish them out to taste them for doneness.

When "done," untie the string and serve immediately on hot plates with melted butter or hollandaise.

Hollandaise Sauce

3 egg yolks
1 to 2 tablespoons fresh lemon juice
Pinch of salt

2 sticks of sweet butter, melted
White pepper, to taste

1. Whisk the egg yolks and 1 tablespoon of the lemon juice together in a small heavy saucepan or the top pan of a double boiler. Add a pinch of salt and whisk until sauce is thick and creamy.

2. Set the pan over very low heat, or over simmering water in the lower pan of a double boiler, and begin whisking immediately. Don't stop until the egg mixture begins to thicken and the whisk's wires begin to leave tracks so you can see the bottom of the pan.

3. Remove pan from heat and begin to dribble in the melted butter, whisking constantly. Use all the butter, but leave the milky part behind.

4. Add white pepper to taste and a spoonful or so of lemon juice.

This sauce will keep, covered, in a warm (not hot) place for at least 30 minutes.

Makes about 1½ cups.

Endive Salad

8 whole endives, trimmed, cleaned,   Walnut oil
   and halved lengthwise   Sea salt
Raspberry vinegar   Rosé peppercorns

1. After washing, place endives in cheesecloth and swing to remove water. Place the endives in a wooden bowl which has previously been rubbed with a clove of garlic.
2. Make a dressing of two parts of raspberry vinegar and eight parts of walnut oil. Season with sea salt and freshly ground rosé peppercorns (mild, sweet, and tangy are available at Zabar's, Broadway at 80th Street, New York City).
3. Chill bowl, dressing, and salad. Mix quickly and serve at once on chilled salad plates. Serve with toasted crisp brioche.

Serves 8.

White Chocolate Mousse

1 pound white chocolate, cut into bits   7 large egg whites, at room tempera-
2 sticks (1 cup) unsalted butter,   ture
   melted and cooled   ¾ cup sugar
7 large egg yolks   1½ cups chilled heavy cream
                                            2 pints fresh sugared raspberries

1. In top of a double boiler set over hot water, melt chocolate, stirring. In a bowl with an electric mixer, beat it for 5 minutes.
2. Add the butter and beat for 1 minute.
3. Beat in egg yolks, one at a time, and beat the mixture for 7 minutes more.

4. In another bowl, using the electric mixer, beat the egg whites until they are foamy. Add the sugar, a little at a time, and beat the whites until they hold soft peaks.

5. In a chilled bowl, beat the cream until it holds soft peaks, and fold it into the whites.

6. Fold in the chocolate mixture, transfer the mousse to a bowl, and chill it for at least 2 hours or overnight.

7. Serve the mousse in stemmed dessert dishes. Spoon some of the raspberries into the bottom of each dish first. Then let it snow.

Serves 12 skinnies or 8 Sydney Greenstreets.

A New Year's Day Menu

Roast Suckling Piglet
Currant and Pine Nut Stuffing
Black-Eyed Peas
Collard Greens
Grandpa Holt's Plum Pudding
Auntie Bellum's Eggnog

A New Year's Day Pig-Out

When Calvin brought the antebellum South to his loft on Canal Street on New Year's Day 1969, it included an ancient black iron stove stuffed with a roast suckling pig, black-eyed peas, and collard greens, and was tended by a mammy right off a vintage Aunt Jemima Pancakes box. For my birthday party on Christmas Eve in the mid-eighties, I wanted to bring back the panoply and pizzazz of that day. My elevator chose to be out of sync, so Calvin braved seven flights of stairs, carrying the grandchild of the piglet of '69. He was followed by Stephen, carrying a case of champagne.

Roast Suckling Pig

1 suckling pig, 10 to 15 pounds   Freshly ground pepper
Salt   1/2 cup vegetable oil

1. Ask your butcher to prepare the piglet, cleaning it, propping its mouth open with a small piece of wood, and slashing the skin on either side of its backbone so that it doesn't swell and burst in the roasting process.

2. Season the piglet's cavity with salt and pepper.

3. Preheat the oven to 325 degrees.

4. Bathe piglet in lukewarm water and dry well with a clean Turkish towel.

5. Fill cavity loosely with stuffing, from recipe that follows.

6. Set pig upright in a roasting pan large enough to hold pig on its stomach with its feet curled under its body. Prop it up with balls of aluminum foil if necessary. Put a small ball of foil in its mouth to hold its shape.

7. Roast for 3 hours, brushing occasionally with oil until the skin is an even golden brown and juices from the thickest part of the pig run clear. If it is browning too much, reduce temperature and cover with foil to prevent charring.

8. For last half hour, baste with pan gravy.

9. Remove to a serving platter. Remove the foil props. Place a necklace of laurel, holly, or mistletoe around its neck, green maraschino cherries or kiwi slices for its eyes, and prop an apple in its mouth, maybe a rose between its teeth, even a bow on its tail. This is a party, isn't it?

10. Serve warm or at room temperature. Carve one side at a time. Try to include some of the crunchy skin with each serving.

Feeds 12 to 18.

Currant and Pine Nut Stuffing

1/4 cup butter   1/4 teaspoon freshly ground pepper
4 tablespoons finely chopped onion   1 teaspoon crumbled sage
4 tablespoons finely chopped celery   1/2 cup currants
4 cups dry breadcrumbs   1/2 cup pine nuts
Salt, to taste

1. Melt butter in a skillet and stir in onion and celery.

2. Cook over low heat until onion is soft.

3. Add this mixture to the breadcrumbs and toss lightly with plenty of salt and pepper.

4. Add sage, currants, and pine nuts and toss again. Stuff pig with this mixture.

Red Wine Pan Gravy

2 tablespoons melted fat from cooked piglet

½ cup burgundy or other red wine
Salt and freshly ground pepper

1. Spoon off all but 2 tablespoons of fat from roasting pan.

2. Using a spatula or wooden spoon, stir and scrape the bits from the bottom of the pan over low heat.

3. Deglaze by adding ½ cup of red wine and cook down quickly. Season with salt and freshly ground pepper to taste.

Use the gravy for basting and also to serve with the pig.

Black-Eyed Peas

1¼ cups dried black-eyed peas
4 cups water

1 cup chopped salt pork
1 medium onion, chopped

1. Put all ingredients together in a saucepan and cook 3 hours or more, at a slow boil.

2. When soft, remove 1 cup of peas, mash well and return to the pan. Add salt and pepper to taste.

3. Serve over cooked rice with greens.

Makes 6 portions.

Collard Greens

1 pound collard greens
1 pound thickly sliced bacon
2 cups water

1 teaspoon sugar
Salt and pepper, to taste

1. Wash collards 3 or 4 times in water, draining each time to get rid of the grit.

2. Strip stems from the leaves. Discard the stems.

3. In a large black cast-iron skillet, brown the bacon. Add collard leaves, stir, and fry until collards begin to wilt. Drain bacon fat, add 2 cups of water, and cook until tender. Add more water if necessary.

4. Add sugar, stirring frequently on medium heat so collards don't burn. Season with salt and pepper to taste. Cooking time is between 20 and 35 minutes.

The greens and peas are a must in the South on New Year's Day. The greens represent dollars and the peas represent change. Eaten together, they promise prosperity for the coming year. The mistake I made on my birthday was to forget the peas and greens.

Serves 12.

Grandpa Holt's Plum Pudding

2 cups self-rising flour
1 teaspoon salt
1 teaspoon ground nutmeg
1 teaspoon ground allspice
1 teaspoon ground cinnamon
1 teaspoon ground cloves
1 teaspoon ground mace
4 cups fresh white breadcrumbs
3/4 cup ground beef suet
2 cups dark brown sugar
3 cups currants
3 cups golden raisins

6 cups dark raisins
1 cup chopped, mixed, candied peel
1 cup slivered blanched almonds
1 large tart apple, pared, cored,
  cubed
Grated rind and juice of 1 orange
6 eggs
1 cup milk
1 cup bourbon whiskey
4 heatproof bowls, 1 1/2-quart capacity
  or 2 bowls, 3-quart capacity

1. Sift the flour with salt and spices into a very large mixing bowl. Add the breadcrumbs, suet, sugar, dried fruit, peel, almonds, apple, and orange rind. Mix. Make a well in the center.

2. Beat the eggs until frothy. Add the orange juice, milk, and bourbon. Pour into the well. Stir until the pudding is thoroughly mixed.

3. Butter the bowls. Fill the prepared bowls to the top. Seal the filled bowls with foil, making them as water-tight as possible. Drape a dampened kitchen towel over each bowl and tie securely with string.

4. Place the filled bowls in large pots that are filled with boiling water coming within ½-inch of the tops of the bowls.

5. Place tight lids on the pots holding the boiling water and puddings.

6. Reduce the heat to its lowest point and steam the puddings 6 hours for the small puddings and 8 hours for the large ones. As the water in the steamer pot boils away, replenish it with more boiling water.

7. When the puddings are done, remove them from the water and let them stand at room temperature. Then remove the towels and foil and re-cover tightly with fresh foil. Refrigerate at least 3 weeks before serving. May be kept up to a year in the refrigerator. Traditionally, they were made a year in advance.

8. To serve, place bowl in a pot and pour in enough boiling water to come about three-quarters of the way up the sides of the mold. Bring to a boil over high heat, cover the pot, reduce heat to low, and steam for 2 hours. Run a knife around the inside edges of the bowl and place an inverted serving plate over bowl. Grasping mold and plate firmly together, turn them over. Pudding should slide out easily.

9. To set the pudding aflame before serving, warm ½ cup of brandy over low heat, light it with a match, and pour it flaming over the pudding.

10. Serve with rum or brandy hard sauce.

Rum or Brandy Hard Sauce

6 tablespoons unsalted butter
6 tablespoons dark brown sugar
Grated rind and juice of 1 lemon

3 tablespoons rum or brandy (or to taste)
⅛ teaspoon ground nutmeg

1. Cream the butter and gradually beat in the sugar with the lemon rind and juice.

2. When soft and light, beat in the rum or brandy a little at a time. Then add the nutmeg.

3. Pile it into a small serving bowl and refrigerate at least 4 hours, or until firm.

Makes 1 cup.

Auntie Bellum's Eggnog

12 egg yolks
½ cup superfine sugar
1 fifth (about 25 ounces) blended
  whiskey or bourbon
1½ cups dark Jamaica rum

2 cups milk
1 quart heavy cream, chilled
12 egg whites
1 tablespoon ground nutmeg

1. In a deep bowl, beat the egg yolks and sugar together with a wire whisk or rotary or electric beater until the mixture is thick enough to fall back on itself in a slowly dissolving ribbon when the beater is lifted from the bowl.

2. With a wooden spoon, beat in the whiskey, rum, and milk. Cover the bowl with foil or plastic wrap and refrigerate at least 2 hours or overnight.

3. Just before serving, whip the cream in a large, chilled bowl with a wire whisk or a rotary or electric beater until it is stiff enough to stand in unwavering peaks on the beater when it is lifted from the bowl.

4. Beat egg whites in a separate large bowl with a clean beater. When firm enough to stand in peaks on beater, scoop the whipped cream over the whites; fold gently but thoroughly together with rubber spatula.

5. Pour the egg-yolk mixture into your best Waterford punch bowl, which has been chilled. Add egg-white mixture and, using an over-under cutting motion rather than a stirring one, fold together with the spatula until no trace of whites remains. Sprinkle with nutmeg and serve at once in chilled punch cups.

Serves 12 auld acquaintances.

A Kosher Wedding Buffet

Gefilte Fish Balls
Fresh Horseradish Sauce with Beets
Kosher Baked Virginia Ham
Roast Turkey
Pickled Cucumber Salad
Potato Latkes
Grandmother Holt's Rose Wedding Cake
Sherried Walnuts

Wines   *Espresso*   *Liqueurs*

Gefilte Fish Balls

3 pounds fish trimmings: the heads,
   bones, and tails of the pike, whitefish, and carp
5 large onions (2½ pounds), 2 cut
   into ⅛-inch-thick slices, and 3
   quartered
4 tablespoons coarse (kosher) salt, or
   substitute 3 teaspoons regular salt
3 teaspoons white pepper

1 pound each of skinned filleted pike,
   whitefish, and carp
2 tablespoons matzo meal
1 egg, lightly beaten
¼ cup cold water
8 medium-sized carrots, scraped; 1
   finely chopped, 6 cut crosswise into
   ½-inch-thick rounds, and 1 finely
   grated

1. Place fish heads, bones, and tails in a sieve or colander and wash them under cold running water. Then transfer them to a heavy 8- to 10-quart pot and scatter the onion slices, 2 tablespoons of the coarse salt, and 2 teaspoons of the white pepper over them. Pour in just enough cold water to cover the fish trimmings and onions, and bring to a boil over high heat.

2. Reduce heat to low and simmer, partially covered, for 40 minutes.

3. Meanwhile, put the filleted pike, whitefish, and carp and the quartered onions through the fine blade of a meat grinder twice. Combine the ground fish and onions in a deep mixing bowl.

4. Chop the fish and onions fine and, with a pestle or the back of a large wooden spoon, mash them into a fairly smooth paste.

5. Beat fish and onions with a spoon until mixture is well blended. Then beat in the matzo meal, egg, the remaining 2 tablespoons of coarse salt, and the remaining teaspoon of white pepper. Beat in ¼ cup of cold water, a tablespoon at a time.

6. Divide fish mixture into 12 equal parts and shape each into 8 round balls, each about 1 inch in diameter. Roll the top of each ball in the finely chopped carrot.

7. When trimmings and onions have cooked their full 40 minutes, scatter carrot rounds into the pot. Arrange the fish balls in one layer on top of the carrots; if they do not all fit comfortably, reserve some and cook the fish balls in two batches. Bring the liquid in the pot to a boil over high heat, reduce the heat to low, cover tightly, and steam the fish balls for 15 minutes, or until they are firm when prodded gently with a clean finger.

8. With a slotted spoon, arrange fish balls on a large platter. Strain remaining contents of the pot through a fine sieve set over a large shallow bowl. Stir the grated carrot into the strained stock.

9. Refrigerate poached gefilte fish balls and strained cooking stock separately for at least 3 hours, until they are both thoroughly chilled and the stock is a firm jelly.

10. Just before serving, chop the jelly fine and mound it on the platter around the fish balls. Spear each ball with a decorative toothpick and serve with a dip of beet horseradish sauce as an accompaniment to any libation from Manischewitz to Piper Heidsieck when you toast the bride or the moment.

Yield: 96 gefilte fish balls.

Fresh Horseradish Sauce with Beets

3 medium-sized beets (1½ pounds)
½ pound fresh horseradish root
4 tablespoons red wine vinegar
2 teaspoons coarse (kosher) salt, or
substitute 1½ teaspoons regular salt
1 teaspoon sugar

1. With a small, sharp knife cut the tops off the beets, leaving about 1 inch of stem on each. Scrub beets under cold running water and place them in a 2- to 3-quart saucepan, adding enough cold water to cover by about 2 inches.

2. Bring water to a boil over high heat, reduce heat to low, cover pan tightly, and simmer till beets show no resistance when pierced with the point of a small, sharp knife. (This will take anywhere from 30 minutes for young beets to as long as 2 hours for older ones.) The beets should be kept constantly covered with water, adding additional water if necessary.

3. Drain beets, cool a bit so you can slip off outer skins. Trim tops and tails. With fine side of a 4-sided hand-grater, grate the beets into a deep bowl.

4. Trim the stem and tail of the horseradish root, then scrape or peel it clean. Grate the horseradish, as fine as possible, into the beet bowl.

5. Stir grated beets and horseradish, then add the wine vinegar, salt, and sugar to taste. Cover tightly and let the sauce stand at room temperature to develop flavor for at least 2 hours before serving. Tightly covered, it keeps in the refrigerator for several weeks.

Makes 1½ cups.

Kosher Baked Virginia Ham

*1 ready-to-eat ham with bone in, pref-
erably from Virginia*
Whole cloves to cover surface of ham

Dark brown sugar
1 can Coca-Cola
1½ cups Manischewitz wine

1. Preheat oven to 350 degrees.

2. Peel skin from ham and trim fat, leaving about a ½-inch layer to protect the meat. With a sharp knife, score fat in a diamond pattern.

3. Set the ham in a shallow baking pan, insert a whole clove in the crossed point of each diamond, and pack the brown sugar evenly over the top and sides of the ham. Pour half the Coca-Cola in the bottom of the pan to prevent the ham from sticking.

4. Bake the ham for 1½ hours (or longer, depending on the size. Consult your butcher to be sure.). Baste frequently, pouring the rest of the Coca-Cola over the ham. After 30 minutes, anoint the ham with half the kosher wine and continue basting. After another 15 minutes, pour the rest of the wine over the ham. Continue to bake and baste from the drippings, wine, and Coca-Cola collected in the bottom of the pan.

5. Transfer ham to a large platter. Skim fat from the pan juices and pour the pan gravy into a sauceboat. Garnish the ham with Peach Pickle (page 113) and Preserved Kumquats (page 114) and give thanks that, yes, Santa Claus, there is a Virginia.

NOTE: This recipe is an adaptation of an old family hand-me-down that traveled by a circuitous route from the chef of the *Normandie*, who basted his ham with Coca-Cola and Burgundy wine.

Serves up to 30.

Roast Turkey

See page 187 for the perfect Thanksgiving turkey.

Potato Latkes

2 large baking potatoes, peeled	1 tablespoon matzo meal
1 small onion, peeled	1 egg, lightly beaten
½ teaspoon salt	4 tablespoons vegetable oil
Freshly ground black pepper	1 cup applesauce

1. Set a large sieve over a mixing bowl and grate the potatoes on the finest side of a stand-up grater directly into the sieve. Using the same side of the grater, grate the onion over the potatoes. With the back of a large, wooden spoon, press as much liquid as possible from the mixture. Discard the liquid and transfer the grated potatoes and onions to a large bowl.

2. Add the salt, several grindings of pepper, the matzo meal, and the egg. With a wooden spoon, beat vigorously until the ingredients are well combined.

3. Preheat oven to its lowest setting. Line a large shallow baking dish with paper towels and place it in the oven.

4. Heat the vegetable oil in a heavy 10- to 12-inch skillet over high heat until a drop of water flicked into it sputters and evaporates. For each pancake, drop 1 to 2 tablespoons of the batter into the skillet and flatten it into a 2- to 2½-inch cake. Fry five or six pancakes at a time for about 2 minutes on each side, or until they are golden brown and crisp around the edges. As they brown, transfer the latkes to the towel-lined dish and keep them warm in the oven while you fry the rest.

5. To serve, arrange the latkes on a heated platter and present the chilled applesauce, if you wish, as an accompaniment.

Makes 12 latkes.

Pickled Cucumber Salad

4 large (8-inch) or 6 medium (6-inch)
  cucumbers
2 tablespoons salt
1½ cups white vinegar

2 tablespoons sugar
2 teaspoons salt
½ teaspoon white pepper
4 tablespoons chopped fresh dill

1. Scrub the wax coating (if any) off the cucumbers and dry them. Score them lengthwise with a fork and cut them in the thinnest possible slices—they should be almost translucent. (There is an item in gadget departments that makes this possible.)

2. Arrange the slices in a thin layer in a shallow china or glass dish and sprinkle with salt. Place 2 or 3 china plates on top of the cucumbers to press out the excess water and bitterness, and let them rest for a couple of hours.

3. Remove the plates, drain the cucumbers of all their liquid, and spread them out on paper towels. Gently pat the cucumbers dry with paper towels and return them to their dish.

4. In a small bowl, beat together the vinegar, sugar, salt, and pepper. Pour over the cucumbers and strew them with the chopped dill. Chill for 2 or 3 hours, and just before serving, drain away nearly all the liquid.

Serves 8.

Grandmother Holt's Rose Wedding Cake

1 cup sweet butter
4 cups flour, sifted 3 times
14 egg whites

1½ cups sugar
2 teaspoons rose extract

1. Preheat oven to 300 degrees. Butter and sprinkle with flour a tube pan 10 inches in diameter by 6 inches high.

2. Cream the butter until it is light and fluffy. Add the sifted flour, a tablespoon at a time, to the creamed butter, beating the batter until it is smooth.

3. Beat the 14 egg whites until they are stiff. Gradually add the sugar, a tablespoon at a time.

4. Fold the beaten egg whites into the flour mixture, a tablespoon at a time. Add 2 teaspoons rose extract.* Pour the batter into the prepared tube pan and bake the cake for 1 hour, or until a straw inserted in the center comes out clean.

5. Leave the cake in the pan for a few minutes and turn it out onto a wire rack to cool.

Serves about 25.

Rose Wedding Cake Icing

2 egg whites
1½ cups sugar
5 tablespoons cold water

1½ teaspoons light corn syrup
¼ teaspoon cream of tartar
Rose extract, to taste

1. In the top of a double boiler combine egg whites with sugar, cold water, light corn syrup, and cream of tartar.

2. Beat mixture until it is blended. Put the pan over boiling water and cook the icing, beating constantly with a rotary beater, for 7 minutes.

3. Remove icing from heat and stir in rose extract* to taste. Continue to beat icing until it is easy to spread, and ice the cake.

Rose Wedding Cake: The Crowning Touch

4 egg whites
1 cup superfine granulated sugar

1 dozen roses, partially closed, and a
*   few rosebuds with stems*

1. In a deep cup or glass, beat the egg whites slightly.

2. Holding the roses by the stems, dip each blossom into the egg whites, sprinkle them thoroughly with superfine granulated sugar, and lay them on paper towels.

3. When roses are dry, remove the stems and arrange the roses on the icing.

* Rose extract, or essence, can be obtained at Kalustyan, 123 Lexington Avenue in New York City, or in Middle Eastern, Indonesian, or Asian groceries in your city. Do not settle for rose water. It is too diluted.

Sherried Walnuts

1 tablespoon butter, softened   *½ teaspoon ground cinnamon*
1½ cups sugar   *⅛ teaspoon ground nutmeg*
½ cup dry sherry   *2 cups unsalted walnut halves*

1. With a pastry brush, spread the butter over a large baking sheet and set aside.

2. Combine sugar and sherry in a heavy 1-quart enameled saucepan and bring to a boil over high heat, stirring until the sugar dissolves. Then cook briskly, uncovered and undisturbed, until about ⅛ teaspoon of the syrup dropped into ice water instantly forms a small ball.

3. At once remove the pan from the heat and add the cinnamon, nutmeg, and walnut halves. Stir gently for a few minutes, until the syrup becomes opaque and creamy. While still soft, spread mixture on the buttered baking sheet and, with two table forks, carefully separate the candy-coated walnut halves. Set them aside to cool, then store in a tightly covered jar until ready to serve.

Makes 2 cups.

An Orgone Box Lunch

If you should find yourself on a riverboat sailing down the Nile or at a performance of Shakespeare in the Park, the menu at hand might be very infra dig. Always remember to check your underwear in case you get run over by a crocodile.

And never leave orgiastic energy to chance. Bring your own Orgone Box lunch and you'll never have to say you're sorry when they hand you a tuna on white with mayo.

An Orgiastic Menu

Oyster Loaf Louisiana Way
A Thermos of Beluga Caviar
Artichokes with Vinaigrette Sauce
Strawberries Romanoff
Bourbon Balls
Splits of Veuve Clicquot

Pack the Orgone Box Lunch in a box worthy of contemplation: an English wicker picnic hamper from T. Anthony, its plastic fittings replaced with Monet porcelain by Haviland Limoges from Tiffany, Puiforcat's Cannes flatware and caviar spoons, Baccarat's champagne flutes, and table (or meadow) linen by Pratesi. Having splurged on the lunch is no reason to stint on the trappings.

Oyster Loaf Louisiana Way

1 dozen oysters
Highly seasoned cornmeal
½ cup corn oil
A baguette of French bread, big enough
  for 2 servings
Butter

Thin slivers of cornichons
Tartar sauce
Nicoise olives
Celery hearts
Radish roses

1. Roll oysters in highly seasoned cornmeal and drop them into hot oil in a heavy, black cast-iron skillet. Fry to a golden brown.

2. Split the baguette lengthwise about an inch from the top to make a lid; make a basket hollow out of the bottom section, leaving an inch of crust all around. (The baguette must be hamper-sized.)

3. Toast the basket and the lid, and butter generously. Put the fried oysters in the basket, along with the slivers of cornichons. Spread the inside of the lid with tartar sauce, and pop it on.

4. Break in half and serve with olives, celery, radishes, and more cornichons.

Serves 2.

A Thermos of Beluga Caviar

If, like Oscar Wilde, you have very simple tastes, and are only satisfied
with the best, then beluga, unadorned, is for you. And a very good place to
find the very best, freshest, at the fairest price is at Caviarateria, at 29 East
60th Street in New York. Be sure to pick up a couple of caviar spoons with
horn bowls at Puiforcat. If you use silver spoons, these extremely delicate
"eggs of the czars" will have a metallic taste.

Artichokes with Vinaigrette Sauce

2 large artichokes, trimmed
1 tablespoon fresh lemon juice
Salt and black pepper
¼ teaspoon onion salt
½ teaspoon crushed black and white
  peppercorns
¼ teaspoon sugar
¼ teaspoon dry mustard
Lemon juice
½ teaspoon Worcestershire sauce

½ clove garlic, finely chopped
1 teaspoon finely chopped onion
1 tablespoon finely chopped, mixed
  parsley, chives, marjoram, tarra-
  gon
½ teaspoon finely chopped green olives
¼ teaspoon finely chopped cornichons
2 tablespoons tarragon vinegar
½ cup olive oil
½ hard-boiled egg, finely chopped

Vinaigrette Sauce:

1. In the bottom of a half-pint, screw-top bottle, put salt, pepper, onion
salt, peppercorns, sugar, mustard, lemon juice, Worcestershire sauce, garlic,
onion, herbs, olives, cornichons, tarragon vinegar, olive oil, and hard-boiled
egg. Shake well. Serve ice cold.

2. To boil artichokes, strip off the larger outside leaves, cut off the stalks,
and trim bases neatly. Rub with lemon to prevent their getting black. Snip off

the end of each leaf with a pair of kitchen scissors within a couple of inches of the base.

3. Remove the inner chokes and tie a thread around the largest circumference of the artichoke.

4. Blanch head-down in fast-boiling water, to which some vinegar, lemon juice, and a little salt have been added. Leave to simmer for 15 minutes. If the leaves will come off easily, the artichoke is fully cooked.

5. When cooked, drain well, dry, and cool. Arrange on a napkin and serve cold with Vinaigrette Sauce.

Serves 2.

Strawberries Romanoff

1 quart sugared strawberries .
½ pint vanilla ice cream
¼ pint whipped cream

Juice of ½ lemon
1 ounce Cointreau
½ ounce rum

1. Place berries in the bottom of a thermos.
2. Whip the ice cream slightly, fold in the whipped cream.
3. Add lemon juice and liquors and pour over the strawberries.
4. Cover thermos to keep berries chilled before serving.

Serves 6.

Bourbon Balls

½ cup chopped raisins
¼ cup bourbon
2 cups chocolate wafer crumbs
½ cup firmly packed dark brown
  sugar

1 cup finely chopped pecans
¼ cup unsulfured molasses
½ teaspoon cinnamon
½ teaspoon ground ginger
¼ teaspoon ground cloves

1. In a small bowl, let the chopped raisins macerate in the bourbon for 15 minutes.

2. In a large bowl, combine the chocolate wafer crumbs, the dark brown sugar, ½ cup of the finely chopped pecans, the raisin-and-bourbon mixture, the molasses, cinnamon, ground ginger, and ground cloves. Mix well.

3. Form the mixture into 1-inch balls and roll the balls in the remaining ½ cup of finely chopped pecans. Store the bourbon balls in an airtight container in a cool, dark place for at least 1 week before serving.

Makes about 36 balls.

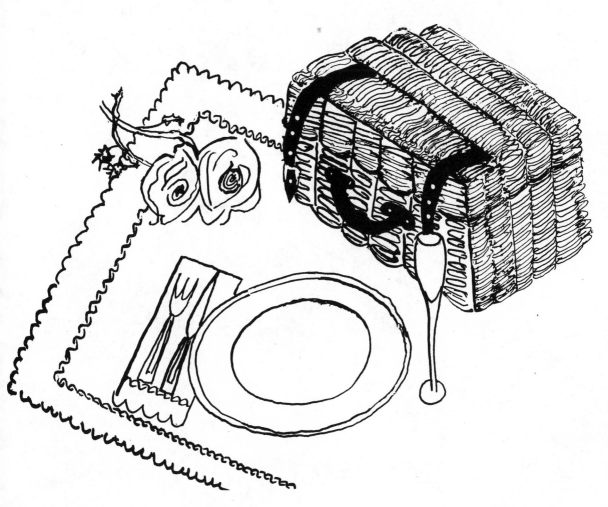

Serious Libations

When Garbo spoke, it was always news. One day she wandered in to discuss antiques with Stephen and Lynn.   Suddenly, a waiter shouted, "There's Garbo," and out she flew. Had she stayed, Stephen would have asked her for a recipe for Swedish Glögg, something you concoct "ven you don't vant to drink alone."

Glögg Garbo

2 quarts Bordeaux wine
2 quarts port wine
½ bottle cognac
2 tablespoons angostura bitters
2 cups golden raisins
Peelings of 1 orange
12 whole cardamoms, bruised in a
    mortar with a pestle or by covering
    with a towel and crushing with a
    rolling pin

10 whole cloves
1 2-inch piece fresh ginger
1 stick cinnamon
1½ cups (12 ounces) aquavit
1½ cups sugar
2 cups whole almonds, blanched and
    peeled

1. In a 6- to 8-quart enameled or stainless steel pot, mix together the Bordeaux, port, cognac, bitters, raisins, orange peel, and the slightly crushed cardamoms, whole cloves, ginger, and cinnamon. Cover and let the mixture stand at least 12 hours so that the flavors will develop and mingle.

2. Just before serving, add the aquavit and the sugar. Stir well and bring to a full boil over high heat. Remove at once from the heat, stir in the almonds and serve the hot *glögg* in mugs. In Sweden, a small spoon is placed in each mug to scoop up the almonds and raisins.

Serves about 20.

Sangria Maria Montez

When the heat's on, climb into a pitcher of the Costa del Sol's preferred beverage. At the Marbella Club, bullfighters and their ladies practically bathe in it to cool down.

Raspberries; strawberries; pitted,
  brandied cherries; brandied peaches;
  fresh pineapple slices, cut in quarters; orange slices; mangos
A few cloves

3 tablespoons sugar, to taste
1 bottle of a full-bodied red wine
½ cup cognac
Ice
1 bottle champagne

1. In a large bowl, place the fruit, cloves, and sugar to taste. Add the red wine and cognac. Cover and let it marinate in the refrigerator for 2 or 3 hours.

2. Pour the wine and fruit marinade into a large pitcher containing ice. Add the champagne. Stir well. Serve at once.

Makes about 6 cups.

Lady Mendl's Punch

1 #5 can unsweetened pineapple juice
1 cup Rose's lime juice
1½ cups vodka, or to taste
8 pineapple chunks

8 thin slices of lime
2 to 3 cups crushed ice
A few drops of vegetable coloring, depending on theme of party

1. In a bowl or pitcher, combine the pineapple juice and lime juice and stir.

2. Fill a 1-quart blender jar half full of the juice mixture. Turn blender on to low speed. CAUTION: Be sure the lid is on when you start the blender. Add the pineapple chunks, lime slices, and crushed ice. Increase speed to high and blend until the mixture begins to freeze (follow the directions under Frozen Drinks, page 150). Add appropriate coloring.

Serves 6 to 8.

Zombie

Meyers dark rum
Light rum
Bacardi Rum

A soupçon of pineapple juice
A soupçon of orange juice

This is the lethal "drink of the walking dead." It is illegal for most bars to serve it in its original proportions (in Boston, the law allows only 2 ounces of alcohol per glass). But at home, when no one's watching, you can fill up a 12-ounce wine glass, at your own risk, leaving room for some ice cubes, a dash of pineapple and orange juices, and that colorful cherry-and-orange-slice "flag" on a toothpick.

Bailey's Comet

1/4 ounce Bailey's Irish Cream   Rocks
3/4 ounce Amaretto

The best thing about this drink is its name. The second and third best things are its ingredients. Pour them over some rocks, stir, and have a liquid dessert with a kick to it.

Sicilian Kiss

1 1/4 ounces Southern Comfort   Rocks
3/4 ounce Amaretto

Aptly named, it's like an offer you can't refuse—on the rocks—mingling two deceptively sweet cordials that could have dangerous consequences.

Peach Cobbler

1 ounce peach brandy   3 scoops vanilla ice cream
4 peaches   A splash of milk

Combine ingredients, blend until thick, and serve in a soda glass.

Godfather

1 1/4 ounces Scotch   Rocks
3/4 ounce Amaretto

In an old-fashioned glass, pour the Scotch and Amaretto over rocks and serve.

Godmother

1¼ ounces vodka   Rocks
¾ ounce Amaretto

In an old-fashioned glass, pour the vodka and Amaretto over rocks and serve.

Rum Runner

¾ ounce blackberry brandy   A splash sweet-and-sour mix
¾ ounce Meyers rum   A splash banana liqueur
A splash each orange juice and pine-   Rocks
   apple juice

Flash blend all ingredients and serve in a 12-ounce wine glass over rocks. (Put in extra splashes of the three juices to fill the glass.) Garnish with a maraschino cherry and a slice of orange held together with a toothpick.

Black Russian

¾ ounce vodka   Rocks
¾ ounce Kahlua

In an old-fashioned glass, on-the-rocks, pour the vodka and Kahlua; stir and serve.

White Russian

¾ ounce vodka   6½ ounces milk
¾ ounce Kahlua   Rocks

In a blender, pour the vodka, the Kahlua, the milk, and do a flash blend (1 minute). Pour over rocks in a highball glass and serve.

Colorado Bulldog

3/4 ounce vodka

3/4 ounce Kahlua

A splash of Pepsi or Coke

6 1/2 ounces milk

Rocks

Pour all ingredients over rocks in a highball glass, stir and serve.

Kamikazee

1 1/4 ounces Stolichnaya

3/4 ounce Triple Sec

1 ounce Rose's lime juice

Rocks

In an old-fashioned glass or in a chilled martini glass, on-the-rocks, pour the Stolichnaya, the Triple Sec, and the lime juice. Stir and serve with a slice of lime.

B–52

1 ounce Kahlua

1 ounce Bailey's Irish Cream

1 ounce Grand Marnier

Serve in a chilled martini glass, floating the 3 liqueurs in the order given by pouring each serving into a spoon, then spooning it over the previous layer.

Planter's Punch

1 ounce dark Meyers rum

1 ounce light rum

1 ounce Bacardi

A generous splash each of pineapple

juice, orange juice, sweet-and-sour

mix, and grenadine

Flash blend all the ingredients for 30 seconds, and pour into a 12-ounce wine glass over rocks with a cherry-and-orange-slice garnish.

Keoke Coffee

3/4 ounce brandy
3/4 ounce dark crème de cacao

Hot black coffee
2 tablespoons whipped cream

In a 12-ounce wine glass, pour the liqueurs and fill with the piping hot black coffee. Stir and serve with a float of whipped cream.

Grand Marnier Coffee

Hot black coffee
1½ ounces Grand Marnier

2 tablespoons whipped cream

Fill a 12-ounce wine glass with hot, black coffee laced with Grand Marnier. Stir and serve with a float of whipped cream.

Milk Train Coffee

Hot black coffee
1½ ounces Bailey's Irish Cream

2 tablespoons whipped cream

Fill a 12-ounce wine glass with hot, black coffee laced with Bailey's Irish Cream. Stir and serve with a float of whipped cream.

Cafe Almond

Hot black coffee
1½ ounces Amaretto

2 tablespoons whipped cream

Fill a 12-ounce wine glass with hot, black coffee laced with Amaretto. Stir and serve with a float of whipped cream.

Irish Coffee

1½ ounces Jameson's Irish whiskey
1 teaspoon brown sugar

Hot black coffee
2 tablespoons whipped cream

In a 12-ounce wine glass, pour the Jameson's, followed by the brown sugar, followed by the hot, black coffee. Stir well. Serve with a float of whipped cream.

Strawberry Fields

1 ounce tequila
1/2 ladle strawberries

2 scoops vanilla ice cream
A splash of milk

Combine ingredients, blend until thick; serve in a soda glass.

Ice Creamed Brandy Alexander

3/4 ounce brandy
3/4 ounce dark cocoa

3 scoops vanilla ice cream
A splash of milk

Combine ingredients, blend until thick; serve in a soda glass with a dash of nutmeg.

Frozen Margarita

1 1/4 ounces tequila
1/2 ounce Triple Sec
1/2 ounce Rose's lime juice

4 ounces sour mix
Crushed ice

1. Combine all the ingredients in a blender and fill with crushed ice to the level of the liquid. Blend until it freezes into a thick smush.
2. Wet the rim of a 12-ounce wine glass and coat it with salt. Fill with the frozen margarita and garnish with a slice of lime.

Strawberry Daiquiri

1 1/4 ounces rum
1/4 ladle strawberries

4 ounces sour mix
Crushed ice

Combine all ingredients in a blender and fill with crushed ice to the level of the liquid. Blend until it becomes a thick smush. Pour into a 12-ounce wine glass and garnish with a whole strawberry.

Banana Banshee

¾ ounce banana liqueur
¾ ounce white crème de cacao
¾ banana

3 scoops vanilla ice cream
Splash of milk

1. Combine all ingredients in a blender and blend until thick as a milk-shake.
2. Serve in a soda glass garnished with ¼ banana slice.

Oreo Express

¾ ounce brandy
¾ ounce dark cocoa
2 Oreos

3 scoops vanilla ice cream
Splash of milk

1. Combine all ingredients in a blender and blend until milkshake-thick.
2. Serve in a soda glass with 1 Oreo.

Grasshopper Pie

¾ ounce green crème de menthe
¾ ounce white crème de cacao
2 Oreos

3 scoops vanilla ice cream
Splash of milk

Combine ingredients, blend until thick, and serve in a soda glass sprinkled with 1 crushed Oreo.

Peter, Paul and Mary

1 ounce Coco Ribe
Coconut
Chocolate shavings

3 scoops vanilla ice cream
Splash of milk

Combine ingredients, blend until thick, and serve in a soda glass, sprinkled with shredded coconut and chocolate shavings.

Black Velvet

A case of Roederer Cristal   *A case of Guinness stout*

Fill the bathtub with ice cubes. Submerge the Roederer and the Guinness, neck up. Have some Baccarat flutes handy and fill them three-quarters full of champagne, topped with one-quarter Guinness. We presume you'll be sharing these bubbles with friends.

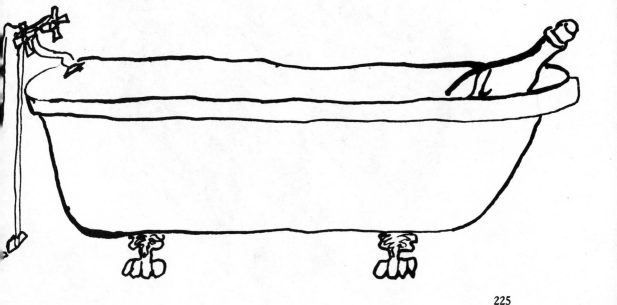

The General Store

(*continued from page 177*)

mane of tawny tresses. She was one of the most photographed of models, Warhol superstars, and social butterflies. Though she was caught by Diana Vreeland in Paris ordering twenty Chanels at a clip (Chanel is Stephen's fashion idol), she paid Stephen the supreme accolade of declaring that he made her the dress of her dreams.

The General Store is a boutique in the most loosely defined sense. It began by selling charming has-beens from attics, thrift shops, Bowery basements, and trash cans. It came to be a browser's heaven to all people of all ages. Its abiding theme was and is the pleasantly unexpected, such as footed cappuccino cups of white restaurant china and eggs of French Limoges porcelain to hold the family jewels, green stamps, or paper clips.

Anita Loos's most serendipitous find was a 46-foot yacht, a small toy boat with 23 pairs of feet dangling from the rudder. This she grandly bestowed on everyone on her Christmas list, whereas Tennessee Williams favored the Hebrew eye-chart dishtowel as the most inspired of house gifts. Gloria Swanson liked to challenge her friends in Tinseltown with the Little Red Riding Hood's Hood jigsaw puzzle, 367 pieces and all of them solid red. Two decades before *retro* (a term coined by *Women's Wear Daily*) became a trend, Serendipity was showing 1920s flapper clothes. It came to be a prophesy, a crystal ball of coming attractions.

To own the latest gag, the newest toy, the most recent Stephen Bruce design was to be one of the avant garde, a privileged circle that boasted such members as model-of-the-year Jean Shrimpton, who appeared on the cover of *Vogue* and in person in Bruce's African-printed Olive Oyl sheath, holding the impossibly tiny "pigeon protector" parasol. Mothers dressed their progeny in sky blue T-shirts awash with puffy white clouds. The passion for "blue cloud T-shirts" extended to the adult market. Soon, there were *knock-offs* (a garment center term for copies) that sold nationwide, and finally from these grew an international trend called "T-shirt dressing."

Every pleasantly unexpected thing that could be carried off, from a Groucho Marx mask to a lightweight waiter, was toted away in the first custom-designed shopping bag in all boutiquedom. It was the newest status symbol, broadcasting the esoteric name everywhere, until all New York got to know its meaning. It dared to clash violently discordant colors, shocking pink and orange. Its motif of the three princes of Serendip was designed by Milton Glaser and Seymour Chwast, founders of Pushpin Studios, the only American design team ever honored with an exhibition in the Louvre. It made shopping bag history, setting a standard for Tiffany's, Bloomingdale's, and a legion of merchants 'round the world to follow. Finally it received its due in a shopping bag retrospective at the Cooper-Hewitt Museum.

Great sport was had lampooning status labels. Gucci, the then "hot" designer Emilio Pucci, and nose-in-the-air Louis Vuitton found themselves called "Goochie," "Poochie," and "Wheeton" on cotton canvas tote bags. Soon the tongue-in-cheek takeoffs rivaled their straight-faced originals for snob appeal. Bruce's name for these carryalls was the final put-down: "Schleppervescence." It shamelessly let the hot air out of Commander Whitehead's "Schweppervescence" advertising campaign with its upper-class British overtones.

The aim was always to get a giggle, to defy the rules of the soulless, killjoy establishment. It was all rather innocent mischief, a little tickle in the ribs, a playful poke at the pretentious, but good clean family fun. Then, in the beginning of the 1970s, they ventured a little farther, and found themselves in a faintly lavender area the faithful fondly referred to as "genitalia."

The pièce de résistance was penis candles. They came in Caucasian, Asian, Red, and Black. They were red-white-and-blue for the Fourth of July. As the howl-of-the-year, they had no equal, and their fame traveled by air, sea, and UPS. A little old lady from Dubuque saw the Caucasian candle and exclaimed, "Oh, what a cunning little pig's foot candle. My daughter would just love it. Wrap it up."

About that time, the East 60th Street Neighborhood Association had begun a cleanup campaign to rid East 59th Street of some trashy newcomers: a house of ill fame and a growing number of fast-food establishments that threatened to spread like a virus. Civic-minded Calvin, always bugging neighbors to sweep sidewalks and get rid of garbage, was in his element. He rose to speak up against vice and junk and was shut up by an outraged local evangelist. "You should talk," seethed the reformer. "You're practically running a porn shop. You sell penis candles, candy panties, explicit Adam and Eve dolls, flasher dolls, the *Weight Loss After Sex Diet Book*." He foamed at the mouth with fury.

Calvin was mortified, a laughingstock. He flew back to Serendipity in a rage, swept all the "offending" merchandise from the counter over Stephen's protests that it was selling like hotcakes, and banished the lot to the basement.

That was February 7, 1971, the night of the New York blackout. There was no electric power, no battery, no candle to be had in all Manhattan. Every restaurant was black and empty. Only Serendipity was aglow with the salacious gleam of penis candles and filled to capacity with rapturous regulars. Resourceful as always, Stephen had had the last word once again.

Next day, the Duchess of Windsor arrived in a chauffeured Bentley. She took one look at the counterfeit dollar bill toilet paper that had surreptitiously been returned to the counter, and squealed, "How much of this do you have? I'll take it all. My friends in Paris . . ."

(To be continued as a Frozen Hot Serendipity Catalogue)

Index

Index

Index

Calvin Holt is the multitalented president of Serendipity 3. He has been a film actor, a modern dancer, and a writer/producer/director. He is an amateur pianist, a watercolorist, teacher, chef extraordinaire, and a television personality. He is good at hog calling, too.

Stephen Bruce does haute with a giggle. His designs have brightened *Vogue* covers and *Harper's Bazaar* pages. He brought hats back into fashion and jeans and cowboy boots into high style. Decorator, floral designer, tastemaker of the Serendipity boutiques, and master of the bon mot, he never climbed the Matterhorn or boiled an egg.

Pat Miller has had a checkered career: As advertising copywriter, she made Levolor a synonym for blinds; a serious painter, she had two one-person exhibitions, two features on "Eyewitness News," and was in numerous group shows. She was managing editor of *The Serendipity Times* and was once a charterboat cook in the Caribbean.